Helene Schellenberg Barnhart

How to Write & Sell the

8

Easiest Article Types

Writer's Digest Books

Cincinnati, Ohio

How to Write and Sell the 8 Easiest Article Types. Copyright © 1985 by Helene Schellenberg Barnhart. Printed and bound in the United States of America. All rights reserved. No part of this book may be reproduced in any form or by any electronic or mechanical means including information storage and retrieval systems without permission in writing from the publisher, except by a reviewer, who may quote brief passages in a review. Published by Writer's Digest Books, 9933 Alliance Road, Cincinnati, Ohio 45242. First edition.

Library of Congress Cataloging in Publication Data

Barnhart, Helene Schellenberg.
  How to write and sell the 8 easiest article types.
  Bibliography: p.
  Includes index.
  1. Authorship. I. Title.
PN147.B325 1985 808'.02 85-3227
ISBN 0-89879-169-3

Book design by Alice Mauro

*To my many students who for more than twenty years
have shared their dreams with me;
your determination and dedication have inspired me;
your friendship has enriched my life.*

HSB

Acknowledgments

No book is ever the product of a single mind. Every author's thoughts reflect ideas absorbed from many other minds. I am grateful to so many from whom I have learned so much.

Much appreciation goes to Louise Boggess, Bud Gardner, and Duane Newcomb, teachers who pointed me in the right direction, and to Lee Roddy who in one of his many talks inspired me to make a written commitment to him to write and finish this book.

Many thanks to the writers who have shared their expertise in the pages of *Writer's Digest* and in *The Writer;* Max Gunther, Omer Henry, Lawrence Block, Louise Zobel, Connie Emerson, Gary Provost, John Brady, Bill Brohaugh—to name only a few.

A special appreciation to the editorial staff at Writer's Digest Books—Carol Cartaino, Beth Franks, and Howard Wells—for their suggestions and constant support through the long days of writing and rewriting.

A big thanks to all my students and writer-friends who generously allowed me to include their experiences throughout the book, and to my agent, Florence Feiler, who is always in my corner.

Helene Schellenberg Barnhart

Contents

12
ONCE MORE WITH FEELING—
FINAL THOUGHTS *201*

The importance of understanding nonfiction technique. When it's all right to break the rules. The philosophy needed for success as a writer. A good support system, where to find it, and how it helps you survive the rough places. How to banish writer's block—the paralysis of not being able to write. The cause. The cure. Your most important asset as a writer and how to guard it. The ultimate joy of being a writer.

Preface

After the publication of my first book for Writer's Digest Books, *Writing Romance Fiction for Love and Money*, I received many letters from writers saying my book had helped them through a writer's block, or had given them hope on a day when they were ready to give up. Writers liked the one-to-one style of the book and they found the chapter "Success Stories"—romance writers telling their own stories—particularly helpful. Then there were letters that came from those interested in learning to write nonfiction. "When are you going to write a book for us?" was the question.

As you know, it doesn't take much arm twisting to get a writer started on a new idea. A few words of encouragement and we're off and running back to the typewriter or word processor. With letters before me from those interested in learning to write nonfiction, I sent off a proposal to the editors at Writer's Digest Books. Happily for you, and for me, they too were enthusiastic about the project.

Writing a book with the purpose of helping other writers is a great responsibility. It is also a humbling experience because of the number of fine books available on how to write salable fiction or nonfiction.

To get myself started and to keep myself going, I relied on the three strong convictions that have carried me through other books and articles.

My *first* conviction is a belief that what others have done, you and I can do. We each have a sufficient measure of talent to enable us to carve out our own niche in the writers' hall of fame. I think of talent as being a feeling for words and a love of putting them together to form images to entertain, to inspire, and to help others.

My *second* conviction is that what you or I have done once, we can do again, and again. With the challenge of each new task comes the needed strength and the ability we need to complete it. We grow as we write.

My *third* conviction comes out of many years of teaching

and working with new writers. I know that any *interested* writer can learn the basic principles of professional technique required to write salable material. The successes of my students have inspired me throughout the years, and the examples of these successes will inspire you.

These three convictions helped me write this book and will help you to achieve your writing goals. What others have done, you can do. What you have done in the past, you can do again. And if you've yet to publish, your willingness to learn the techniques in this book will take you a long way toward your objective.

Helene Schellenberg Barnhart

Off to a Good Start— Putting the Odds in Your Favor

By choosing to learn how to write and sell nonfiction, you've put yourself far ahead of many other writers who haven't yet defined their goals. The nonfiction market is wide open to any writer who has something new to say about an old subject, and to one who has the imagination and foresight to grab a new idea and run with it.

To prove the predominance of nonfiction over fiction, take any magazine off your coffee table, open it up and look at the table of contents page. What do you see? Articles outnumber short stories. My latest copy of *Good Housekeeping,* for instance, lists two fiction pieces and a dozen articles. And one of the two fiction selections is by a big name writer, a condensation of Arthur Hailey's *Strong Medicine.*

Family Circle states in its guidelines, "Occasionally uses fiction." An issue of *The New Yorker* contains one fiction piece and eleven articles. *The Saturday Evening Post* usually has one or two short stories sandwiched in among a generous supply of articles. Many magazines don't use fiction at all.

There's a reason for the popularity of nonfiction in today's magazine marketplace. Publishing companies spend huge amounts of money surveying readerships to learn reader preference. The surveys reveal that today's reader wants to be informed. The world is changing so fast that yesterday's miracle is today's accepted fact. People no longer must wait days, weeks, or months for the news of change to reach them. News is at their fingertips with a flip of the TV or radio dial.

But television and radio can give news only in capsule form—bits and pieces of what's happening in the world. Once interested, the viewer wants to know *more,* and turns to the pages of a magazine or newspaper for additional information. To the surprise of many in publishing, television and radio have motivated people to read more, not less. Readers like their information in all kinds of packaging. Some like neat, tidy packages—information given in a straightforward, no-nonsense manner. Others like a package with a big red bow—information given in an entertaining manner, with possibly a touch of humor here and there.

YOU—THE SOURCE

Without you, the writer, white space remains white, just as the computer screen remains blank until ideas are fed into the disk. You are the source from which the world of publishing draws its life. The unpublished writer today becomes the published writer tomorrow. Editors spend a good part of their days, and even their nights, searching through mountains of submissions to find manuscripts that are fresh and exciting in point of view and that reflect professionalism.

Think of yourself as a professional at all times—someone of extreme importance to the publishing world. Keep in mind that the difference between the selling writer and the nonselling writer is not so much a matter of talent as it is of learning a few fundamental techniques for professional writing.

If you have yet to make your first article sale, this book will push you that much closer to the day when a long, slim envelope containing a check will replace one holding a rejection slip. If you are selling articles in one or two categories, reading and studying this book will help you broaden your base. Where you've been selling to one or two editors, you can sell to many.

The title of this book reflects two concepts important to your success as a writer. The first concept is how to write, and the second is how to sell what you write. Too often the writer thinks of these as separate and unrelated. The two functions, writing and selling, are as closely bonded as are Siamese twins at birth.

From the moment you get an idea you think would make an interesting article, consider who will want to read what you write. Once your article is written, it becomes a product to be sold in a competitive marketplace. The more people who are interested in reading what you write, the more possibilities you'll have to market your product, and the fatter will be the check.

To evaluate the *salability* of your article idea, ask yourself if the subject matter is of universal interest. By *universal*, I mean that your subject affects the lives of all kinds of people everywhere. We all have certain needs that must be met if we are to survive happily.

Universal Needs

Food We must eat to live.

Housing We all need shelter of some kind.

Love Life without love is barren, a wasteland. Babies deprived of loving attention sicken and die.

Faith Every culture has its own spiritual beliefs in a Power outside of self.

To Belong Even as children we feel a need to belong. Being a member of a family, a church, an organization, or a profession gives us a sense of identity as to who we are.

A Sense of Accomplishment Most of us feel the need to fulfill a purpose for the privilege of taking up time and space in this world. Whatever form it takes, accomplishment gives meaning to our lives.

Recognition Whereas a sense of accomplishment comes from within, recognition comes from outside ourselves. Whether we like to admit it or not, most of us hunger for recognition of our worth. When we do something well, we like to be told. Such expressions as "perks" and "carrots" reflect the importance of the need for recognition.

There are other needs that psychologists tell us must be met if we are to enjoy life. To mention a few more universals, we have the need to:

Be healthy

Feel secure

Find an expression for our creativity

Find a way to self-improvement

Use leisure time to enjoy the fruits of our labor, and money to buy a few basic necessities as well as simple pleasures.

Understanding the importance of these human needs will contribute to your success as a writer. Each one of these universal needs lends itself to not one, but many articles you can write and sell.

YOU, THE EXPERT

You don't need a string of degrees in front of your name to become an expert as a writer. It's what you know, or what you *learned* from an experience, and your ability to pass on this knowledge that makes your article potentially salable. Ann Landers, Dear Abby, and Helen Bottel have become famous because their columns speak on the problems evolving out of universal needs that for some reason haven't been satisfied—falling in and out of love; selling a home and moving far away to a strange neighborhood; confusion over identity; loss of respect; growing up without ever knowing parental love.

Take food as an example. You may never have known what it's like to starve, but chances are good that you know what *too much* food does to you. Losing and gaining weight is a subject that never grows old where magazine articles are concerned. Vegetable gardening, cooking and serving food are just a few of the other possibilities for articles on the subject of what we put into our mouths and stomachs.

As you read and study this book, have a notebook handy into which you jot down the key points of each chapter. For your first entry, I suggest you list the *universal needs* that motivate human behavior. Take each of the needs and write a sentence or two describing some experience you've had with it. You'll find as you do this exercise that one or two of the needs and the experiences you had will "turn you on." When you feel that excitement and enthusiasm, tag that entry as a good possibility for a salable article.

GET A HANDLE ON IT

When you get an idea that makes you want to run to your typewriter, stay the impulse to start writing. A little pre-typewriter planning will save you wasted hours later.

An idea is not material for an article until you give it a "handle," a focus on one special phase of your subject. You can't write everything you know about food, or housing, or love. Not in one article. You must break your subject matter down into one area of interest. If you take dieting as your focus, even that is too broad. Narrow "diet" down to one particular kind. (As an example, you might write an article describing how you lost weight eating only six days a week. I have a writer friend who claims that's how he lost 65 pounds and kept it off.)

EIGHT WAYS TO GO

When you have a handle on your article idea, you're ready to consider which treatment would be best for your subject. Which *kind* of article will you write? You have *eight* possibilities. They are:

1. The personal experience article
2. The profile article
3. The inspirational article
4. The how-to article
5. The nostalgia article
6. The travel article
7. Think and humor articles
8. The mini article

As a reader you've enjoyed each of these eight article types over and over again. They constitute the nonfiction backbone of magazine and newspaper publications.

I call these articles easy to write and easy to sell because in over twenty years of teaching writing classes, I've watched many beginners become professional writers with their by-lines above one or more of these eight types of articles. You'll meet many of these successful students in this book.

In discussing each of the article types, I back up theory with published examples taken from my bulging files. These examples will show you how you can take your ideas and fit them into one of the article categories.

If you're a writer still hoping to make that first sale, consider each of the article types carefully. Don't be afraid to experiment with several different ones. By learning to write more than one kind of article, you'll create a secure place for yourself in the nonfiction marketplace, and you'll increase your writing income.

Mastering the requirements for each type of the eight articles isn't difficult because *all* articles have a common foundation. Building a nonfiction article is like building with blocks.

The Construction Business

The first block is *the lead,* a few sentences or a short paragraph that will immediately grab the reader's attention. For example, this could be the lead for an article on alcoholism: "Are you a secret drinker living in terror because you're afraid your friends or your boss will find out?" Such a lead gets the problem out in the open and grabs the attention of anyone seeking help. It also identifies the reader.

The lead I've just given you is a *question* lead. There are several other types for you to choose from in setting up your articles. The lead you select depends upon the type of article you're writing and also on the emotional impact you want to make on the reader to get his or her attention. Here are some possibilities in addition to asking a direct question.

The dialogue lead. An example in a parent-child relationship article might be, "I'm not going and you can't make me," declared my rebellious ten-year-old daughter, Jenny.

"You're going—even if I have to carry you," I replied firmly, taking her by the shoulders and pushing her toward the door.

This dialogue lead is a good one to set up characterization and to hint at the problem. We know from what the child says that she's defying her mother. The mother (the narrator) is obviously intent on holding her ground. The reader's suspense is aroused, and he or she will want to read on to see what caused this stand-off.

The startling statement lead. Example: "Despite billions of dollars spent on research and law enforcement, drug abuse by America's kids continues on an epidemic scale. . . ." (From "Kids and Drugs" by Tom Kunci, *Woman's World,* December 11, '84)

The quotation lead. Example: "Sticks and stones may break my bones but words can never hurt me," is an old adage many of us chanted in childhood. When we grow up and become adults, we learn words *can* and *do* hurt us.

This is the lead I plan to use in a proposed article (still on the back burner) on the destructive power of carelessly chosen words whether written or spoken. I feel the familiar saying pinpoints the theme of my article idea.

Anecdotal lead. Example: An article from *Woman's Day,* December 11, '84, entitled, "The Best Medicine Can Be You!" by Maggie Strong.

"Our children were ten and eight the summer we got the diagnosis: My husband Ted had multiple sclerosis. We told them Daddy had a balance problem—that's why he had been walking so slowly. We told our friends the facts. When you have MS, the linings of the nerves disappear. . . ."

This lead goes into an anecdotal account of how the author explained to her children and to her friends what had happened to her husband. The lead continues for another paragraph with further description of MS in a quietly accepting way. This prepares the reader for the body of the article, which shows the kind of help needed at such a time.

Case history lead. Example: An article in the January 17, '82, *San Francisco Sunday Examiner* entitled, "Victims: How They Lived, How They Died," compiled by staff writer Mike Lassiter.

"Lester Eugene 'Gene' Rumrill, 47, and Yvonne 'Vonna' Blount, 32, were avid outdoors people. Rumrill taught classes in wilderness studies for the University of California at Santa Cruz's extension and had founded its Sierra Institute. . . ."

The lead goes on to profile not only the character and lifestyle of Rumrill and Blount but also gives a case history kind of description of numerous other victims who were in the wrong place at the wrong time and were murdered.

The *case history* lead is effective for exposé articles because it provides background material on the subjects prior to the main event that the article focuses on. Case histories as they might appear in police files or in those of a doctor are a means of giving a lot of information in the fewest possible words, details necessary to the reader's understanding of the problem which unfolds in dramatic form after the case history.

Description lead. Used often in travel articles, it sets the geographical scene giving place and time. Example: A travel article in the December 9, '84, *San Francisco Examiner.* "Dickens Lives On in London at Christmas," by Neil Morgan, a prolific travel writer.

"London—Charles Dickens will roam the streets of London again this Christmas. I swear it. At Christmases past I have followed him through narrow winding streets whose people he knew well. You might find Dickens entering Garrick Club in Covent Garden, little changed from the days when he was a member . . . or the Athenaeum Club in Pall Mall. . . ."

The lead goes on to describe all the places where Dickens can still be found in spirit and sets up a typical Christmas scene in London—today.

Try these different kinds of leads in your articles. When just the right one falls into place, you'll know it. It will feel right because it fits your story.

The second building block is the *premise.*

Having caught the reader's attention with a forceful lead, you, the writer, must state clearly and simply how you feel about the problem or situation. To return to our example of secret drinkers, is it safe for an alcoholic to come out in the open? Is there really help for the disease?

You might use the following as your premise:

> If you're a secret drinker, afraid to admit you have a problem, you're not alone. There are thousands like you, afraid to come out of the closet, but desperately wanting help. The help you seek is there, waiting for your phone call.

The third building block in any article is the *body,* usually the middle portion where solid backup information is given to support the premise. In order to have a firm foundation for the body of an informative article, you must do careful research. You can't support your premise with a few facts written off the top of your head. You need quotes from authorities, statistics that bear out the truth of what you say. For a personal problem or inspirational article you may need case histories showing how others solved the problem.

Your research into background information on the article on alcoholism could require a visit to AA (Alcoholics Anonymous) and other organizations dealing with the problem. You'd talk to doctors who specialize in the treatment of alcoholism and get permission to quote them directly. You'd talk with alcoholics and their families and try to get some poignant quotes relative to how they feel about the problem.

While the lead grabs attention and the premise makes your position on the subject clear, it is the *body* of any article that proves to the reader you know what you're talking about. It's the convincer.

Transitions are the fourth building block without which an article would wobble. Transitions are phrases and sentences that provide little bridges over which your reader crosses to get from one idea to another. Transitions move the article along from point to point.

A few transition phrases you might use are:

1. Another aspect of the problem is
2. In talking with several doctors on the subject
3. According to the latest survey
4. There are several ways in which we can
5. Looking at the problem from the viewpoint of

Each of these examples is a key phrase which leads into a further discussion of the subject. Each one prepares the reader for something new to come.

The fifth building block found in all article types is the *conclusion,* the final wrap-up of the subject, summarizing what has been said throughout the piece. One final new point is often made in the conclusion—an additional insight for the reader.

The sixth and last building block or element in the structure of your article is the *theme,* or the insight for the reader. If, in your premise, you promised help for the alcoholic, then in your theme you would state in strong terms your conviction that no one with a drinking problem need fight the battle alone. Your theme message might be:

> The best way to get help with any problem is to admit we need help. Those around us don't know how much we suffer until we cry out. Help is there waiting—just on the other side of the closet door. But only *you* can open the door.

There you have them—six building blocks that provide any type of article with a firm support. List these six important elements in your notebook, and when you write any kind of article, check it against your list. With these in mind, you're ready to take on the not-too-difficult task of learning the individual characteristics of each of the eight easy-to-write-and-sell article types.

WRITING ON PURPOSE

As with any endeavor, wanting to learn is half the battle. Determination will carry you a long way toward Publisher's Row. There's another special trait that will help you succeed in the article-writing field, and that is a desire to help other people. Whatever kind of article you decide to write, ask yourself: *In what way will my article help someone solve a problem? How will it enrich people's lives? What is the purpose of my article?*

Every article, whatever kind, must have a purpose. You have several choices. You can *inform.* You can *inspire.* You can *entertain.* You can *make people think.*

It's possible in any article to have a dominant, or primary, purpose and a secondary one. For instance, you might *give information* in a serious, in-depth way that might also (secondarily) motivate people to think about the problem or situation, even to take action.

You could give the same *information* in an *entertaining* vein, making your serious (secondary) point through satire or humor.

As you learn about each of the eight article types, you'll see the different ways in which a writer can take an idea to the reader. At the end of each chapter you'll find a checklist to help you make sure you've covered all the important elements for that particular article type.

As you read and study the following chapters, you'll find exciting ideas for different kinds of articles you want to write passing through your mind. You must capture these ideas before they float away into oblivion. Think of your notebook as your net. Once inside, the idea is in safekeeping for future use.

Your notebook already has two important lists, one the *universal needs* from which you can draw countless salable article ideas, and the other the *six building blocks* you'll need to create a firm foundation for whichever kind of article you decide to write. You might now add the four general *purposes* of articles: to inform, to inspire, to entertain, and to make people think.

Learning to write is much like learning to drive a car. You can think about it and talk about it, but it isn't until you get behind the wheel that you gain the confidence to turn on the ignition and go!

You've got the key in the ignition. Your notebook is handy. You're all set now to learn to write and sell one of the most popular kinds of articles—the personal experience.

Adventures in Living—
Writing the Personal
Experience Article

I f you're like many people, you've been writing about your personal experiences most of your life. Probably the first personal experience you wrote was done at the equivalent of sword's point—an assignment in grade school to write about "What Happened on My Summer Vacation."

In the years following, you wrote letters telling family and friends not only about your summer vacation, but about all your other adventures: your first job, falling in love, getting married, your first child, the first home of your own, and a myriad assortment of other experiences.

Perhaps you kept a diary or journal in which you jotted down daily happenings and how you felt about them. Or you may have worked on your high school or college paper or yearbook, and written profound essays, or your observations on life.

As an adult, you may have shot off letters to the editor of your local newspaper in which you aired your views on what you considered deplorable situations in your town. Or you may have taken issue with some article published in the paper or in one of your favorite magazines and written a rebuttal.

TURNING PRO

Childhood compositions, diaries, journals, letters—all make an excellent apprenticeship for your present goal, that of writing salable personal experience articles. There is one big, important difference, however, between those earlier attempts and writing professionally. In those early writings, you wrote to satisfy some deep personal need. The piece you wrote on your summer vacation helped you get a passing grade. Writing in your diary allowed you to confide in a trusted friend when you needed a sounding board. (Dear Diary would never tell.) Letters to friends gave you a chance to share complaints or good news. Epistles to the editor gave you an opportunity to let off steam in a simple letter-writing form.

If you wrote well, family, friends, and neighbors complimented you. If you were dull, those around you were too polite to say so. You were spared the sight of your great effort being scanned and then tossed into the nearest wastebasket.

So far, nobody paid you a dime for your literary masterpieces. It was all for free, so you could write as you pleased. Now things are different. Now you want to write and get paid for it; you want to publish what you write. With this goal in mind, you can no longer cater to your own feelings, your own whims. Your purpose in writing has changed, and that requires a change in attitude toward your writing.

Writing for Readers

In writing for publication you write not only for your own satisfaction, but to share your experiences in the hope of helping someone else. Your own emotions are important, but equally important are the feelings of your reader. What you experienced must mean something to your reader, must provide information, inspiration, entertainment, or a mixture of all three.

In evaluating the experiences you've had in terms of potential for a salable article, keep your reader in mind. It is not enough that you, your family, and a few intimate friends find humor, pathos, inspiration, or any other emotional element in your experience. Your family and your friends *know* you, and that adds interest to your telling of the experience.

The reader, on the other hand, does *not* know you—except through the words you put on paper. To make up for this gap, the experience you use as a personal experience article must have *reader identification.*

Reader identification means that what happened to you has an element of universality, something all kinds of readers recognize (reader identification), such as the loss of a loved one, a difficult parent-child relationship, or coming to terms with aging.

Your purpose, then, in writing about what happened to you is to help the reader in some way—to show how you coped, how you learned a certain technique, or how you survived a life-and-death situation. The reader may not be called upon to handle a similar crisis, but he or she will take away from your article a lesson in courage and faith, as well as an example of ingenuity. The lesson will perhaps help the reader through his or her own problem—whatever it may be.

Don't be discouraged if you've never had a dramatic life-and-death experience. Many published articles are based on everyday happenings. What makes the experience interesting to others, and therefore salable, is the *interpretation* you give to the experience—the fresh insight you gained from it.

IS ANYBODY READING?

Your insight is the magnet that pulls the reader into your article and provides the take-away element. The particular kind of take-away you give the reader depends on the kind of experience you had, the market, and the readership. Your article must be written in such a way as to meet *the specific needs of a very specific readership.*

Meeting readership needs is called slanting, which means that you have a definite picture of your reader in mind. When you have selected a certain experience from your life for a possible article, ask yourself two important questions before you begin the first rough draft.

1. Who is my reader? Age? Education? Economic status? Social interests? Religious/political beliefs? Write a one-page profile of your prospective reader.
2. How will my article about my personal experience help my reader? In what specific way? Inspire? Inform? Instruct?

With a good profile on your readers and a clear picture of the way in which your article will help them, half the work of writing is done.

Finally, keep in mind the lessons you learned from your experience. Did you gain a more positive attitude toward life? Did it help you to understand human nature better? Did it give you a new set of values—did a catastrophic happening, in which you perhaps lost many material possessions but those you loved were spared, teach you how precious life is, and how fragile?

Any lesson drawn from your experience can be passed on to the reader through a well-written article. By well written, I mean an article well structured with a strong opening paragraph that sets the scene of your experience and the kind of experience (humorous, tragic, shocking), followed by a solid body (middle portion) with plenty of dialogue and action to give dramatic interest, and a conclusion that clearly states your theme—the lesson you learned, a lesson that readers will find helpful in their lives.

Personal experience articles fall into four categories: humor, adventure/action, psychological, and inspirational. You're sure to find a type to fit your experience(s).

EXIT LAUGHING

Humor is always salable. In Chapter 8, I'll discuss humor writing as a category in itself, but the humorous personal experience relies mostly on the character of the experience rather than on the writing. The experience was downright funny, and the reader's reaction will be anything from a broad smile to a hearty laugh.

Editors are always on the lookout for a well-written humorous experience to balance what might otherwise be heavy content. All kinds of magazines use humor in some way—even if it's only a brief filler inserted somewhere on a page of other kinds of material.

Reader's Digest has several sections devoted to humorous fillers. In the February '83 issue half a page of fillers about inconvenient visits from unexpected callers appeared under the heading "Door Stops." The following filler from "Door Stops" was submitted by J. L. Jones:

> Friends of ours who had just bought a freezer decided to get a side of beef and cut it up themselves. They cleared the kitchen

table and set to work with saw, knives and cleaver. The couple was wrestling with the huge carcass when there was a knock on the kitchen door and the new minister peered in.

"I was just calling to introduce myself," he said, "but I see I'm interrupting your meal, so I'll call again."

We all can remember a minister or someone we might want to impress, coming to call and catching us unprepared and perhaps at our worst. Again, a universal subject. We identify with the situation presented in the filler. (In Chapter 9, you'll learn more about fillers, as well as other short articles you can write.)

A humorous full-length personal experience article written by Maynard Good Stoddard was published in the July/August '84 issue of *The Saturday Evening Post.* The title clues us into the kind of reaction we can expect to feel—a smile, a chuckle, or even a good hearty laugh. Title: "Putting My Best Foot Crosswise."

The blurb also sets the tone. "Why should anyone buy ski equipment and travel clear to Aspen when he can break a leg just as easily in the comfort of his own home?"

If there's any doubt left in the reader's mind as to the kind of personal experience he's about to read, the lead quickly melts away the confusion.

> I had interrupted my wife's evening monologue, something about knitting a scarf for the neighbor's cat, to read the staggering prediction that there will be four and a half million home accidents in our country this year.

We're already smiling at the description of the scarf-knitting for the neighbor's cat.

The wife's reaction broadens our smile. "Let's move," she said.

The author then goes on to give us hilarious descriptions of the kinds of home accidents he encountered with skate boards, stairs, ladders, a can of spray paint wedged in his pocket, and so forth.

The conclusion keeps to the same light-hearted, tongue-in-cheek humor:

> A playboy acquaintance of mine who heard I was working on this piece almost had me convinced that the best way to avoid home accidents is to show up at home as seldom as possible. The other day when I met him he was sporting a black eye. So there goes that.

End. Exit laughing. Reader take-away.

What's So Funny?

Never has the world needed laughter more than it does now when we're inundated on all sides with tales of death and destruction from poverty in the less fortunate countries and from a possibility of nuclear war. Day after day, we read screaming gloom-and-doom headlines. Sometimes, it's almost more than we can bear.

Laughter is the safety valve in the pressure cooker of our lives. Often the only thing that keeps us going is the brief moment in which we chuckle over some amusing anecdote in our favorite magazine or newspaper, or share a funny personal experience, one of those "Wait 'til you hear this one. You'll-never-believe-what-happened-to-me-yesterday—" stories.

The need to smile, to laugh, or to burst our sides once in a while is something all human beings feel. *The New Yorker* magazine recognizes this need by sprinkling many of its serious-minded pages with cartoons guaranteed to get a smile or even a belly laugh. *The Saturday Evening Post* has its cartoons and its Postscript page of humorous asides and verses. *Reader's Digest* contains several monthly humor sections. You'll find the recognition for the need for humor in all but a few publications.

With this need in mind, sort through your *funny* experiences and try to capture their humorous essence in a short article that will bring a smile or a chuckle from readers desperately needing escape from the pressures of their lives.

INTO THE WILD BLUE YONDER

The adventure/action personal experience article is distinguished by its highly dramatic subject matter and style of writing. Not every adventure/action story is about a life-and-death struggle, but all articles of this type must contain that breathless moment of suspense in which you (the writer) find yourself in an exciting *physical* contest of some kind.

The purpose of the adventure/action article is to give the reader a vicarious thrill as you, the writer, fight off anything from a swarm of bees to a herd of rampaging elephants, or as you demonstrate your skills of survival in anything from a leaky canoe caught in the rapids to a single-engine plane on final approach in a dense fog.

Reader interest in adventure/action articles is sustained through the excitement of the dangerous situation, the resourceful ingenuity of the participant, and by the inspirational examples of courage and faith that bring about the final satisfying ending: a safe landing, escape, or winning over seemingly hopeless odds.

An exciting example of an action/adventure personal experience appeared in August '84 *Reader's Digest*, originally published in *Geo*, February '84. Titled "White Water Run on the 'Eater of Men' " and written by David Roberts, the title programs us for plenty of thrills, such as:

> The veteran leader of our rafting expedition chose to walk around the most treacherous rapid of the wild New Guinea river. But when we were about to lose a boat, he responded in a most improbably swashbuckling way.

There are harrowing moments in this personal experience of rafting 75 miles down the Tua, which is described in such adventure-filled sentences as:

> Ahead of our farthest downstream camp lay rapid after rapid as turbulent as the last one, culminating in the suicide canyon.

The concluding dialogue summarizes the danger for those who take on the challenge of such a venture.

> "We underestimated it," Bangs [expedition leader] told me. "I doubt anybody will ever navigate the Wahgi-Tua-Purari system from top to bottom."
> Then he smiled. [Characterization.] "But who knows?"

In action/adventure articles, as in short stories, you must plant and foreshadow coming events. Give the reader examples of the important dominant character trait that will help you or another character in the experience survive or win.
Bangs is described earlier as "a white water 'wild man.'"

> Tall and sandy-haired, Bangs looks more like a coffee-house intellectual than a rugged outdoorsman. But when faced with a challenging river, he becomes totally determined.

Determination, then, is the dominant character trait the author has chosen to give us, one that will establish the credibility of this man's courage and stamina in the action/adventure scenes. Reader *take-away* is in the vicarious thrill of sharing such an adventure through reading the article.

SECRET SELVES

The psychological personal experience article depends more upon inner conflict than it does upon outer, physical action. Psychological personal experience articles show the author, or someone close, coping with personal and family traumas and life crises.
A good example of this type of psychological personal article is one titled, "I Don't Drink Cocktails Anymore," by Alanson B. Houghton, a former rector of the Church of the Heavenly Rest, New York City. (Originally published in *The Episcopalian Jubilate Deo,* reprinted in August '84 *Reader's Digest.*)
The lead hooks us into the problem situation of the personal experience immediately.

I was a two-drinks-before-dinner man. For over 30 years, those cocktails had been a daily ritual.

The author then shows us how he gave up what he thought of as an "unproductive habit." In the conclusion, he sets his theme with

The last thing I want to do is sound pious, for everyone is different. But for me, giving up an unproductive habit meant gaining something far greater, something I didn't realize I'd lost. I have a renewed sense of control over my life, and a renewed sense of love.

Reader take-away in this article is found in the encouragement the author gives through his own experience in quitting the cocktail habit.

Psychological personal experience articles must have many examples of the positive winning out over the negative. Hope replaces despair. Doubt is replaced by faith. Practical easy-to-follow suggestions should be included in the article to start the reader on his or her way to coping or overcoming.

To succeed with this popular type of article, you must genuinely care about people. You don't mind opening your heart to strangers—if it will help someone solve a problem or survive a difficult situation.

Start your psychological article in the negative, a black moment in your life in which you felt something of value slipping away. In the body of your article, show yourself struggling to find the answer to a problem, or a way out of a situation. Use plenty of emotion, plumbing the depths of *your* feelings. Dramatize with use of dialogue and action. Conclude with a strong theme, a statement of what it was exactly that pulled you through. Point out to readers that they can win using the same skills or positive attitudes that helped you.

WORDS TO LIVE BY

Most inspirational personal experience articles published in religious magazines such as *Guideposts* provide the reader with a specific kind of take-away, that of a *spiritual* experience. These articles often dramatize a moment when faith is tested, and the climax shows faith in a Higher Power winning.

Characterization and identity of a so-called Higher Power in inspirational articles depend on your selection of markets. In denominational publications such as those published by the Baptists, the Catholics, and the Lutherans, the definition of the Power beyond human experience reflects the rituals, the symbols, and the beliefs of each particular denomination.

A nondenominational publication, such as *Guideposts,* is read by people of all faiths and therefore the editors are careful not to slant the identification of Higher Power to any particular religious sect. Readers are left to interpret Higher Power according to their own particular religious belief. Such words as God, Jesus, Virgin Mary, Saviour, etc., are often missing entirely or are used sparingly in order to establish identification with a wide cross-section of readers of *all* religious or philosophical beliefs.

We'll go into the how-to of writing and selling this type in Chapter 4. For now, let's look at how other personal experiences, those thought of as *art of living,* can inspire readers.

Carol Amen launched her writing career with the inspirational or art-of-living type of personal experience articles. Whatever happened to Carol in her daily life she held up to the light, and if she found that important element—potential for helping someone else—she wrote about it. Because of her warm, helpful style of writing and her obvious integrity, reader response to Carol Amen's articles was impressive. Readers wrote from all over the country telling her how her articles had helped them cope.

One article, "Hyacinths to Feed the Soul," was reprinted by *Reader's Digest* after it appeared in a religious magazine.

"Hyacinths," like other Amen articles, was based on a seemingly undramatic everyday event. As a student nurse, Carol had earned extra money by baby-sitting. One night, she sat for a young couple who wanted to get away from their two children for a night on the town. Carol observed from their home that they were not rich. When she blurted out that the evening would be expensive, the young husband answered, "I guess it will. But it's important to us to have some time to ourselves. We're both tired and snapping at each other."

Ardeth, the wife, smiled at Carol. "Don't you know about hyacinths to feed the soul?" She took a volume of poems from a shelf and showed Carol a poem written by Sadi, a Persian sheik who lived more than 700 years ago. The poem read:

> *"If of thy mortal goods*
> *thou art bereft,*
> *And from thy slender store two*
> *loaves alone to thee are left,*
> *Sell one, and with the dole*
> *Buy hyacinths to feed the soul."*

The lesson from the poem, and the example of the young couple putting the poet's words into action, stayed with Carol. Eventually that personal experience took her all the way to a sale to *Reader's Digest.*

Carol Amen's advice to new writers of inspirational articles goes like this: "Avoid sounding condescending or too profound. You have to plop yourself right down in the mire with the rest of the human race, and then you show yourself figuring out a way to get out. You have to be willing to expose yourself in a bad light at first, and then catch onto the theme or the message that someone (like the young couple I baby-sat for) reveals to you. You must show how the experience changed you."

In her article, "Hyacinths to Feed the Soul," Carol Amen dramatized the negative attitude that can cause unhappiness when in dialogue she has the young husband confess that he and his wife had been snapping at each other. They needed a night out.

Carol reflects her own unawareness in her comment that the night out would be expensive.

The positive element or *change* begins when the wife opens a book of poems so Carol can read "Hyacinths to Feed the Soul." The poem reprinted in the article is the turning point—for the characters in the article, for the author, and for the reader.

Reader take-away in an inspirational type article is a fragile thing. It takes much practice in order to skillfully blend in the theme or the lesson to be learned. Readers don't like preaching. They want their lesson to come through a moving and highly inspirational dramatization of an event in someone else's life, an event that was the turning point.

Browse through your own moments of inspiration, those moments when you felt either a Divine Power, or some other force outside yourself coming to your rescue. What was it that brought you out of dark despair into the light of hope? Was it something someone said? Was it something you read? Was it the display of courage and faith of a loved one or a close friend?

Whatever inspired *your* moment, write it down, everything you can remember about how you felt before, during, and after the moment of change. Such a memory could be the starting point for your article.

Once you capture the essence of the inspiration for your article, learning to write the article isn't difficult. Inspirational writing may be one of the most satisfying types of writing you can do.

The next chapter will give you the simple and easy-to-learn steps in writing an inspirational article. Bring your experience along with you so that you'll be ready to start what might be your first inspirational article.

WRITING THE LEAD, BODY, AND WRAP-UP

Most personal experience articles start with a strong lead in which a clue is given to the type: humorous, adventure/action, psychological, or inspirational. In the May '84 issue of *Guideposts,* an article by Lee Ann Cowen entitled, "Mama—What a Beautiful Word," begins with the desperate tone needed for a "survival" personal experience story.

> I raced the car through the near-deserted streets toward the hospital, trying to swallow the panic in my throat. I dared not look toward the passenger side where Ken held our two-year-old son's limp body against his chest. *"Patrick, please don't die,"* I thought wildly.

The action word, *raced,* along with such phrases as *the near-deserted streets, trying to swallow my panic,* and *our . . . son's limp body . . .* all build up the life-and-death drama of this experience. The lead sets the note of urgency required.

"Patrick, please don't die" draws the reader into the story because the words again dramatize desperation, thereby creating intense suspense for the reader. Readers identify with the mother and with the child. They must read on to find out what happened.

A good lead raises questions in the reader's mind. This lead, setting up the desperate situation, does just that.

Most writers like to get their lead set before they go too far with the writing of their articles. Since the ending circles back to the lead, having the lead fixed in mind helps tremendously in planning the body and conclusion.

Practice writing leads. Start with a simple, straightforward declarative sentence but make sure the sentence contains at least one word or phrase that will create the emotional response you want your reader to feel.

In the body of your personal experience article you present the complications you faced in your particular experience. As in a short story, no complication should be overcome unless a new one has begun, and the biggest complication of all is dramatized in the crisis scene.

In planning the body of your true experience article, use your work notebook to list all the complications you encountered in the experience you're writing about. Plan how many short scenes you'll need to present these complications. You may find that you can combine two or three in one scene, whereas a particular complication may need an entire scene to dramatize fully.

The complications must support the dramatic impact of the lead. The complications in the article "Mama—What a Beautiful Word" are a good example of how this element can intensify reader suspense even more.

The *first* complication in Lee Ann Cowen's poignant article comes when she tells us, "This was Mother's Day. How odd. It seemed impossible that this quiet gentle afternoon could have erupted into anything so awful."

The *second* complication comes when the author describes how she started the car (flashback) and then heard her husband screaming, "Stop!"

The *third* complication is presented in a description of the car door flying open and Ken, the author's husband, leaping into the car holding their son's crumpled body.

Complication number *four* comes through a graphic description of how the author met her husband's eyes and knew that she had done the unthinkable. "I had hit my son."

Other complications follow when the police arrive and ask searching questions that add to the author's feeling of guilt. Then there's the uncertainty of the outcome. Will Patrick be brain damaged? Will he live? There's the complication built into the long wait through surgery and afterwards. We're told that days passed. Patrick hung on.

The agony of the situation is spelled out in these complications as the parents await the outcome.

The reader lives this experience with the author and her husband, and when the joyous moment comes when the child opens his mouth and says, "Mama," the reader experiences the same sense of relief and gratitude as felt by the parents.

Once the goal has been reached, the story is over. Tie up any loose ends, and in your best writing state the theme—the lesson learned, the insight gained through your experience. The wrap-up should circle back to the beginning to give the reader a final glimpse into how it all started, and to show how far you've come since then. Whatever the nature of the experience you had, it must have left an indelible impression on you, and in turn, the reader gains a new insight.

The personal experience article, "Mama—What a Beautiful Word" leaves an indelible impression on the reader through its upbeat and meaningful ending. Patrick recovers and goes home. There's no brain damage and no physical limitations.

The author tells us, however, that *her* scars did not go away as Patrick's did. The sense of guilt lingered. The author then tells us she prayed. "Help me too."

Her prayers are answered when Patrick winds his arms around her and says, "I love you." It is the child speaking, but to the mother it seems to be God's love, a love that went beyond a child's. The words bring a healing.

The theme is an inspirational one spelled out in these words: "No matter what we've done as parents—the big mistakes and small, intentional or unintentional—God understands and still counts us worth loving."

The reader identification is strong in this article. We all can visualize how heartbreaking it would be to run down your own child. We *feel* for the mother. We want the child to live and be whole again, and we want the mother to recover from the pain of such a tragedy.

The ending in this beautifully written account of a mother's harrowing experience leaves us emotionally satisfied.

SECRETS OF SUCCESS

Whatever kind of personal experience you choose to write about, it must be of such a nature that it left an indelible impression on you. You gained a new insight.

It is through the warmth and sincerity of your style that you transfer the indelible impression *and* the new insight on to the reader. The reader lives your experience vicariously through your words, feeling your emotions whether they are those of joy or anguish.

Before you write that final draft of your article, go over it one last time to make sure it has all the essential ingredients:

- A strong element of truth
- A once-in-a-lifetime feeling
- A warm and intimate style
- Strong reader identification
- Vivid dramatization
- An emotional take-away for the reader.

Take a moment to jot down these vitally important elements, using index cards or your work notebook. Let's examine each element to see how it fits into the structure of the personal experience article and how you can use each to full advantage.

Truth

In telling about your experience, you're allowed to change the identity of other people to protect their privacy, and you can alter the location, or disguise it, for the same reason. You can dramatize, that is, create conversations you may not actually have heard, or are unable to recall verbatim. The one thing you must not do is fake the experience itself.

If you make up an experience, or if you stretch the truth too far, you'll lose the integrity of the honest emotion that can only come out of an actual experience. It's the sharing of a genuine emotion that allows the reader to live the experience with you.

In some types of personal experience articles, there is a confessional quality in the style, but personal experience articles must not be confused with so-called confession-type stories such as those found in *True Story* magazine. Confession stories are *based* on actual events that happen in real life— usually taken from accounts told by friends and family, or from newspapers, but the story itself is fiction—fictional characters, events changed around to suit dramatic requirements and plot needs.

Confession writers play many parts. When I was writing confessions, I (fictionally) was a mixed-up teenager, a disillusioned war veteran receiving a Dear John letter, a husband wanting a sex change operation—you name it. It was only the essence that I drew from life—the real event or the real character was never used. I always took the viewpoint of the victim rather than the active participant, the one who was hurt by the trauma and so went off the deep end for awhile, got into trouble, saw the light, and shaped up. I was once the wife of a man condemned to the electric chair. The wife's "sin" was in spending all her money and her child's on trying to prove her husband's innocence after he was dead. She didn't believe the jury. But she found evidence of his guilt in the Bible he left his son—a message, "God forgive me," written in the margin. It was a real tear jerker. All fictional, but inspired by the story of a killer condemned to the electric chair.

I repeat: The event about which you write in a personal experience article is real. It happened to you, or to someone close to you.

Editors have sharp eyes when it comes to anything phony in a piece of writing. If the editor finds your personal experience was a fake, you'll lose your credibility as a writer and will have a hard time publishing anything.

Once in a Lifetime

Whatever your experience was—tragic, poignant, or hilarious—it must have left an indelible impression. Your experience changed you in some way. You may have had this experience years ago, but it is as fresh in your mind as though it happened yesterday. It was not the magnitude of the event itself that made this a once-in-a-lifetime experience, but the emotional impact it had upon you. So before you write your experience article, think about the dominant emotion you felt at the time you lived the experience. Write that emotion down in your notebook.

You build your article around this one emotion. If you write well, your reader will laugh with you, cry with you, experience spine-tingling fear or whatever emotion you felt when you had the experience. Success in writing personal experience articles comes in having your reader vicariously live your experience, feeling what you felt as it happened.

Intimate Style

When you sit down to write your personal experience story, whatever type it may be, pretend you are sitting at the kitchen table confiding in a close friend. Your reader *is* this friend and you're pouring out the incredible experience you had.

33

In the verbal telling, because of the emotion the experience brought (the indelible impression), you use simple language. Your sentences are short. Your verbs are strong. You pause often. You break off. You clear your throat and start again.

In writing the experience, you must use these same devices to build the emotion. Simplicity. Brevity. Action verbs. Pauses or transitions. Write simply and honestly in an almost conversational style.

With the exception of using strong action verbs to dramatize, use everyday words that are quickly understood by everyone. So-called "highfalutin" language gets in the way of emotion. If a reader has to stop and wonder what a particular word means, you've lost him because you've pulled him out of the experience he is vicariously experiencing.

Dramatization

In writing personal experience articles, you borrow the fiction writer's technique. You create action scenes. You use generous portions of dialogue. You characterize. Rather than merely recounting that the doctor told you that your husband had only an hour to live without the operation, you let the doctor speak for himself. In addition, you characterize him briefly, so that the reader has a mental picture. For example:

> Dr. Holmes, a tall, rangy man, looked at me gravely. "We have no choice, Mrs. Clarke. We've got to operate."
>
> I drew in my breath. "And if you don't operate?"
>
> "Joe won't survive more than an hour."
>
> Dear God! An hour to live—unless. But the operation had never been done before . . . etc.

In this example, you can see the re-creation of the moment of decision through the use of description and dialogue. The dialogue is brief, the way people talk when under stress. Simple, everyday words are used. Again, people in emotional life-and-death situations speak tersely and in simple language.

come a problem and a situation. Show the reader how the experience changed you. As you survived and learned, so can the reader.

4. Keep your writing unpretentious and open.
5. Show, don't tell. Dramatize as you would in a short story, building short scenes of action and dialogue.
6. Select a dominant character trait that will motivate the turnaround for yourself or another person involved in the personal experience.
7. Read the kind of personal experience articles you'd like to write. Keep your colored pens and pencil handy to underline the various elements, such as dialogue, characterization, conflict, vivid description. There isn't any better way to learn to write than by reading and studying good models.
8. Make daily entries in your notebook about your experiences—even your dreams. Who knows? Someday the telephone may ring and it may be a Hollywood agent wanting to buy your personal experience for a film.
9. Keep mailing. Never overlook a small, seemingly unimportant market. Your personal experience article, like Carol Amen's, could end up in *Reader's Digest.*

CHECKLIST FOR YOUR PERSONAL EXPERIENCE ARTICLES

☑Is there a strong element of truth? Does the story sound as though it really happened to you?

☑Does your experience carry that once-in-a-lifetime feeling?

☑Have you written in a warm and intimate style?

☑Have you *dramatized* the scenes in your personal experience? Used plenty of dialogue and action to create vivid word pictures?

☑Do you feel that the reader will *identify* with your experience? Is there something *familiar* that the reader will recognize?

☑What is the take-away for the reader? Is it inspirational? Practically helpful in solid suggestions given to help the reader avoid your mistake(s)?

Fascinating
Characters—
Writing the Profile
Article

H aving read and studied the chapter on personal experience articles, you may not feel ready to write about yourself. If so, the profile article may be just the place for you to start. Profile articles are about other people.

THEY'RE EVERYWHERE

I was introduced to profile writing when I was Woman's Page editor on a Northern California newspaper, the *Pacifica Tribune*. My boss thought it would be a good idea if we showcased interesting women in the community.

"Do a profile a week," was the order.

New on the job and never having written a profile before, I was scared spitless. The deadline to fill the empty white space was two days away. Observing that my face paled at the thought of going out and finding my first profile subject, my boss took pity on me and gave me an assignment.

"This woman has an interesting collection of early American antiques," he told me. "Find out how she got started collecting, what's so special about the collection, and anything else you can dig up about her hobby that'll make a good profile. Our photographer will go with you and take her picture."

It wasn't until he gave me the woman's name and address that I relaxed—a little. The owner of the interesting antique collection was my neighbor. Someone I knew. She lived across the street from me. I had talked to this woman many times. I knew about her collection. But it wasn't until I was sent out on the assignment to write a profile on her that I realized material for an easy-to-write article lay right at my doorstep. I telephoned my neighbor for an appointment, and explained to her that a photographer would be with me to take her picture.

The interview went well in spite of my nervousness, and the next week my first profile appeared in the paper. My neighbor was a celebrity, and that profile was the beginning of a series that ran for the next two years—one a week. Before I finished my stint on the local paper, I'd interviewed all kinds of interesting people: VIPs at City Hall, members of the clergy in all denominations, the queen of the beauty pageant who later was a runner-up at the state level, and my favorite, a woman who was foster mother to five Down's Syndrome children.

WHAT IS A PROFILE ARTICLE?

When a portrait photographer or an artist wants to capture one side of a person's face only, he has that person sit so as to let the light fall on just one side of the face—the profile.

In the same way, a writer can *highlight* a particular area of a person's life. The profile article is not a cradle-to-grave account; the writer zeros in on his subject in relation to a specific activity or circumstance. Overcoming a handicap, coping with a crisis, coming to terms with changes such as the empty nest and retirement are situations offering material for profile articles. Hobbies and professions that are filled with adventure or are different from the usual types of occupations make good profile material, too. Profiles on celebrities are always popular; you can even write profiles on historical figures.

If you're new to writing profiles, start with someone you know; someone with whom you'll feel comfortable. Don't know any interesting people? Think a moment. Like my neighbor with the early American antique collection, your subject could be right next door, or even someone in the family.

Remember, you're looking for someone with one colorful, interesting, and exciting activity, hobby, or absorbing interest. You'll know you've got potentially good material when you discover this person devotes most of his or her time to this one activity. Show how the hobby or activity enriches the subject's life—this is the take-away for the reader.

Hobbies and activities are not the only possibilities for profile material. Watch for people who have overcome seemingly insurmountable physical and psychological handicaps to reach a goal.

Someone in your town or county has made an amazing recovery after a near-miss with death. What pulled him/her through? In the answer to that question lies your profile story.

We all love to read about people who have courage, unshakable faith, persistence, and determination. Such people inspire us when we are faced with our own breaking point.

I've mentioned two kinds of profile material: the hobby or activity category, and the recovery or overcoming handicap type. There's a third type that focuses on some major contribution that a single person or a group of people make to society. For instance, MADD, Mothers Against Drunk Drivers, is a group organized out of one mother's grief and desperation when her child was killed by a drunk driver. Similar organizations have sprung up to deal with other heartbreaking problems that plague modern society: child abuse, the battered wife, alcoholism, drug abuse, cancer, heart disease, the homeless—the list goes on and on.

This kind of profile requires an in-depth treatment and exhaustive research. It isn't as easy to write as one focused on a happy activity such as quilt making, or an exciting activity such as hang gliding or scuba diving. Even the profile centered on one person's recovery from a critical illness or one who is living successfully with a handicap is less difficult than the social-problem story. But these profiles attract a wide readership because social problems concern us all—few families are spared the unhappiness of at least one type of trauma.

WHERE DO I FIND A SUBJECT?

Your local newspaper is one of the best sources for stories that will get you started writing profiles of people not in the public eye, past or present, but who for some reason are exciting to write about.

The sports section, the calendar of events, the woman's page are a few of the specialized sections of your daily paper that can provide you with excellent material. Don't overlook the business and financial pages.

Watch your daily newspaper for news items about people in your community who are active. Buried in the account of a woman who is to chair a certain charity project may be the information that she is a doll collector, or likes to hang glide in her spare time, or is an accomplished artist or musician. People who are active in social and community projects are usually equally absorbed in some personal hobby, craft, or activity.

As an example of what you can find in special sections of your daily newspaper, a glance in the back-to-school section of my local paper today yielded a profile on a woman principal who was retiring after twenty-five years in education. The profile centered on the many changes she'd experienced since the days when she taught in a one-room school warmed by an oil stove, with a yearly salary of less than $3,000.

An even more in-depth story could be written on this woman for such magazines as *Parents, Redbook, Good House-keeping,* and many others. For *Parents,* a profile could be done on how she feels about "spare the rod and spoil the child," or one focusing on her suggestions for preparing a child for first day at school.

How does this woman feel about teaching as a career for women in today's world? Such an article would have potential for *Woman's Day, Family Circle* or *Woman's World.*

What about her retirement plans? How does she feel about closing the principal's office door for the last time? The retirement magazines, such as *Dynamic Years* and *Modern Maturity,* might be interested in such a story.

In the same paper appeared an appealing picture of a woman holding a cuddly koala bear. The caption beside the picture reads, "Hanging in There," and the brief text tells us that Blinky Bob, the koala, is one of San Diego's two dozen koalas. Vickie Kuder, the woman holding the adorable Blinky Bob, works as a keeper in the zoo.

What's it like to work in a zoo? Why did Vickie choose such a career? Does she become personally attached to the charges under her care? Two koalas have died lately, the account informs us. A third is found to have traces of the fungi suspected in the deaths. Isn't such a situation hard on someone working daily with the koalas?

This one photo of the koala and keeper starts a trend of

thought that could end in not one but several profile articles with different markets in mind, such as juvenile publications, Sunday supplements, trade magazines, and of course, all kinds of family type publications.

Other Sources

Weekly church bulletins can be a gold mine of source material for salable profiles. For instance, you read that a bazaar is scheduled at a certain church. There will be a raffle drawing on a beautiful handmade quilt created by a member of the congregation.

What an exciting possibility for a profile story. Quilt making is almost a lost art. Once it was the focal point of social life in rural communities, when women gathered to visit and innocently gossip as they worked at quilting bees.

The woman who has made the quilt or inherited it is undoubtedly full of information about quilts. A profile on her and her quilt would find a ready market, not only in craft and hobby magazines, but in women's and family type publications as well.

In researching sources for profiles about people with interesting hobbies and skills, don't overlook various kinds of fairs, such as Renaissance, State, Home and Garden fairs and shows. Also, believe it or not, flea markets can turn up some colorful profile material. Going to flea markets and staking out a table or booth at one has become a cult, with "regulars" traveling miles to attend or take active part in flea marketing. Such events are meccas for talented people who create all kinds of interesting products, from prize-winning jams and jellies to model airplanes, as well as those who collect antiques and other conversation pieces.

Another source of profiles about everyday people can be found by listening to conversations going on around you wherever you happen to be—in a carpool, on a bus, train, or plane. You never know when your antenna is going to pick up on some fascinating story in someone's life that you could use.

CELEBRITIES—ALIVE AND WELL

So far, I've talked about profiles you can write of living people, those you know personally and those you come to know through the methods I've suggested.

There's another completely different article you might like to write, the profile about a person you may never meet, but in whom you have a great interest.

A friend of mine, Dianne Kurlfinke, has written a series of successful articles on male movie stars, most of whom she never met. She's published profiles on such movie greats as Tyrone Power, Jimmy Stewart, and Rudolph Valentino. In each profile she managed to catch a fresh facet of the movie star, although each had been written about many times before.

In the Tyrone Power piece, her fresh angle was the fact that Power's good looks were actually a handicap in his career. He wanted to be taken as a "serious" actor. In her touching profile of the movie star who was "too handsome for his own good," Ms. Kurlfinke tells how Power was eulogized at his death as "a beautiful man." Little was said of his acting talent.

From her exhaustive research into the lives of her favorite male movie stars, Dianne Kurlfinke discovered a fresh theme she could use in her profiles. The men who were the perfect lovers on the screen, such as Power, Gable, and Valentino, were not destined to know bliss in their real-life romances. Also, the role into which they were cast was not always the one they would have chosen.

You may be wondering how you could ever aspire to write about movie stars when perhaps you live hundreds of miles from Hollywood. Do as Dianne Kurlfinke did—read everything you can about your favorite movie star or other celebrity—biographies, publicity releases, and other profile articles. Read with the idea of finding a new dimension to the celebrity's personality or life. You'll have to dig. There may be only a sentence or two that serves as a clue. You build on this small clue, finding other sources that reinforce the idea. Gradually, the substance of the article you want to write will form.

As for illustrations—photographs of the celebrities—you

can obtain these through promotion and publicity depart-ments of different studios. You may have to pay for some pho-tographs; others will come free. Ms. Kurlfinke obtained her pictures of Tyrone Power and other movie stars through the Museum of Modern Art/Film Still Archives.

LATE GREAT SUBJECTS

Most historical figures have been written about many times. What chance have you, then, to write still another profile arti-cle on such well-covered subjects as Abraham Lincoln, George Washington, or Helen Keller?

If you can find a fresh twist or slant, something other writ-ers haven't thought of, you have a good chance to find a mar-ket for your story on familiar figures of the past.

As an example, if you found out that George Washington told a lie, or stretched the truth a bit, you'd have a fresh profile, one that emphasized George's human side.

Irving Stone found a new slant on Abraham Lincoln when he researched the life of Mary Todd Lincoln. He came up with a woman's view of the man, a story quite different from that of the historical and political version.

If you're a history buff, you'll like researching and writing about famous people of the past. Keep your eyes open for clues that can lead you to a completely different slant on a fa-miliar historical figure. When you find one, you'll feel the ex-citement of a prospector who, panning for gold hour after hour under a broiling sun, sees a glint of gold in his pan.

There are times when clues are hard to find in your search for background material on your profile subject. Your research librarian can be a life-saver at such times, directing you to the musty dusty tomes in the "back room" for some let-ter, journal, news clipping, or out-of-print book that contains a nugget of information you can use for your article.

You might have to invest some money in a research trip, traveling to the village, town, or city where your profile sub-ject lives or has lived. Such an investment usually pays off in the unexpected surfacing of research material you thought you'd never find.

Irma Whipple, a writer-friend, made four trips to Germany in an effort to track down background material for her book, *In Search of Familie Wiese*, a history of not only her family roots back to the sixteenth century, but also an account of the immigration of a whole group of people from Germany to America. After self-publishing her book, Irma found herself a popular lecturer on the subject of researching ancient archives.

"There was only one missing link," she tells her audiences. "The missing link was Uncle Julius."

To fill in the gap in her family tree, Irma and her husband drove up to Alaska where it was said Uncle Julius lived for a while in his nomadic life. They learned from library research that to find the story of Uncle Julius, they must contract for a plane and a bush pilot to take them to a distant outpost not accessible by road. Undaunted, they got the pilot and plane and winged away on the final leg of their search, a successful one in that they actually found an old-timer who remembered Uncle Julius well and filled them in on him.

You may not be ready to hire a bush pilot and plane and go zooming off into the wilderness, but do try to get as close as you can to your profile subject's world—even if it means spending some money and time. In your travel research, you'll not only find missing clues on the profile you're writing, but also rich source material for countless other articles.

RESEARCH RULES

In doing any type of research, whether it's for a profile on your neighbor down the street, or one on someone who lived several hundreds years ago, check and recheck your facts. Keep careful records of where you find your information. Use your notebook to jot not only the author (if you're researching articles and books), but the publisher and date of publication. It helps to keep a record of the exact page on which you found the entry.

The same rule applies in talking with living people about a possible profile subject. Keep a record of the day the conversation took place, whether in person or by telephone. Avoid wasting time going back to double-check information you're not sure of in an interview by using a tape recorder. A tape recorder used properly (make sure it's working) is proof of the exact conversation.

Research Sources

Almost every town of any size has a genealogical and historical society ready to help you in your research. The genealogical archives kept by the Church of the Latter Day Saints in Salt Lake City is open to those searching their roots and has a seemingly inexhaustible supply of records on not only Mormon families but also on a great number of non-Mormons.

Genealogical and historical societies collect and keep family letters, journals, and photograph albums donated to them by generations of people who have lived in the area. You are welcome to browse through these treasured sources telling of bygone days and those who lived in another time and another world.

Your library is not only a source of written material for articles, it can also give you contacts for future interviews through the bulletin board that lists the names of coming speakers.

Chance conversations, your daily reading, and television and radio talk shows can all serve as research sources, giving you the first glimpse into an interesting person's life and providing basic information upon which you can build through the other sources I've mentioned.

GETTING STARTED

We'll assume you've found your gold nugget, a fascinating person you can write about. You've stumbled on a few exciting facts about this person, and you want and need to know more;

much more. Where and how do you start?

Take a living person, someone you know, because, as I said earlier, it's easier to write about someone close to you.

You have some before-hand information through personal association, or through an item you read in your local paper. You're ready now for the second phase—the interview.

SETTING UP THE INTERVIEW

The first step is to make an appointment, a definite time and place for the interview. If you don't have your subject's telephone number, you can usually find it in the telephone book, through your newspaper, or perhaps through some organization mentioned in a write-up you have seen.

If for any reason you can't get a telephone number, write a letter to your subject and address it to him or her in care of the newspaper in which the news item appeared. If someone tells you about an interesting interview possibility, naturally, you'll get the subject's telephone number and address from that source.

In one way or another, you've obtained the telephone number. You're ready to set up an appointment. Always explain that you are a writer and you're interested in doing an article on him or her. If you have other credentials, mention them. No need to explain you've never published anything—if such is the case. If you are a published author, by all means tell your subject.

In setting up many appointments during my two-year stint of writing profiles for my local paper, I found it helpful to suggest a choice of two times when I'd be free to do the interview. This technique makes it easy for your subject to make a choice. If neither of the two dates is convenient, of course you reach for a third possibility.

Avoid the I-can-come-over-anytime approach—even if the subject is your aunt Martha. Your time is valuable. In most cases, your subject will happily select one of the times you suggest as convenient.

When making the interview appointment, tell your subject how much time you'll need. Most profile articles run from 1,200 to 2,000 words, so you should be able to get enough material in an hour to an hour and a half. If the interview runs on and on, you lose the freshness required to capture a sharp portrait study of the person. In knowing ahead how much time you need, your subject has a chance to clear the decks so that you two can be alone to concentrate on the interview.

Tactfully suggest the need for peace and quiet. Such questions as, "What is the best time for you? Perhaps you'd like me to come when your children are in school" (if this is appropriate), or "Perhaps we could have lunch together"—to free the professional or business person from office interruptions.

However you do it, get across the idea that you need time *alone* with your subject. Nothing kills a good interview like constant interruptions, telephones and doorbells ringing, children running in and out, and so forth.

Getting the Picture

Most profile studies need photographs to dress them up. I was fortunate in having the services of my paper's photographer. Many writers doing profile articles take their own pictures.

Once you get interested in writing profile articles, as well as other types, it's a good idea to take a course in photography. Such classes are available through your adult education program and through your local college. The class fees are nominal and will be well worth the time you spend learning the basics of good photography.

Always let your subject know in advance (at the time the appointment is made) that you'll be taking pictures. Most women like their hair and makeup to be at their best, and men like to be free of five o'clock shadow.

In taking the pictures that will accompany your article, try to take action shots or environmental portraits, that is, pictures showing your subject in relation to the hobby, activity, interest, you'll highlight in your article.

With few exceptions, it is better to take black and white

pictures. They are easier and cheaper to reproduce in newspapers and in most magazines. As to size, most editors prefer 8x10 photographs. You'll find tips on how to submit photographs and the type desired in your monthly issues of *Writer's Digest* and *The Writer,* and also in *Writer's Market.*

DO YOUR HOMEWORK

Good interviewers spend time researching what interests the people they are going to write about. The preparation you make for your interview *before* you meet your subject helps you tune your inner ear to catch hidden facets of your profile's life. As you play your tape after the interview, incidents your subject related take on added meaning because you've taken the time to learn about his or her past.

In preparing for your interview, focus on the aspect of the subject that you intend to highlight in your profile. Keep in mind the *portrait* angle I mentioned before. You article will be centered mostly on a single feature of your subject's life. It might be a hobby or a skill. It could be an activity, as for instance, the mother who was instrumental in founding the organization against drunk drivers.

Whatever it is that your profile subject does that is exciting and different, *that's* what you'll highlight. In order to do a good job of bringing this facet to the foreground, you must know something about it yourself.

Where do you get this information? You get it in exactly the same places you get information on any subject; in books, in talking to other people who also do whatever your profile does so well, in visiting appropriate museums and art galleries.

Once you have a grasp of the topic that is the focal point of your profile's life, you're ready to jot down some questions. You'll be primed to interview the person in an intelligent and informative way. When your profile sees you know a little about what's so exciting to him or her, he or she will open up and be eager to tell you *more.*

Having a list of questions that show you're truly interested and well informed will do wonders when you're in that face-to-face confrontation. The fact that you cared enough to be well prepared will create trust and rapport. "What was it like growing up as a boy on a sheep ranch? Did you do much drawing in that one-room schoolhouse? Did you like to dance as a child? Is it true your mother took you to Hollywood when you were just a youngster? Your father was a marine biologist. Is that why you decided to go into oceanography?"

One word of caution. As much as possible, avoid looking down at your notes. Go over the questions several times so that they are fresh in your mind. Your questions must appear to be spontaneous and unrehearsed—a natural upwelling of a genuine interest in what turns your profile on.

As in all other types of articles, it is the *emotional* response you get from your profile that will put the shine to your piece. Your genuine interest and eagerness to learn more about what means so much to your subject will provide the "highlighting" you need, a light that will shine in your profile's eyes and smile as the story unfolds.

Think of yourself as a photographer when you set the stage for your interview. Shine the light of your own interest and knowledge on your subject and you'll come away with material for a "life-like portrait."

FACE TO FACE

On the day of the interview, dress with care, wearing whatever you think will be appropriate to the occasion. Women who spend most of their time at home, mothers with small children, and retired people might feel more comfortable with you if you appear in more or less casual attire rather than dressed like a high-fashion model.

Remember, your subject (unless a celebrity) is just as nervous as you are. It's your job to put him or her at ease as quickly as possible. A warm smile goes a long way, as does a friendly handclasp.

A sincere compliment when you enter a home, an office,

or any other interview setting, can break the ice and create instant rapport. Glance quickly around the room and note some object that is obviously important to the person you're about to interview.

"What a lovely rose. Is it from your garden?"

"What a gorgeous view! You can see the Golden Gate."

"What a pretty child!" nodding toward an obviously prized photo.

People's homes and their offices are more than just places where they eat and sleep and do business. Homes and offices are mirrors that reflect personality, tastes, dreams, and loves. Entering a lawyer's or banker's office, you might see a photograph of the subject taken on a fishing trip. Beside the man stands a boy or a girl. And the catch, the fish, the subject of many a tale. A comment on the picture will loosen the tongue as nothing else could.

Once you're settled down for the interview, sometimes at the kitchen table, sometimes before a cheery fire, sometimes across a cluttered desk or in the gloom of a garage or workshop, begin the interview with simple, easy questions, such as "Have you lived here long?" That leads to a question about where the subject lived before the move. Questions about the family might be in order if there are children still around.

Although these preliminary questions are more or less intended as a *warm up* to relax both you and your profile, often an exciting bit of information is unexpectedly uncovered that will add dimension to your article. You might find out, for instance, that your subject hadn't thought about painting, sculpting, rock hounding, bird watching (or whatever it may be) until an illness or accident created unexpected free time.

This type of revelation might lead to an interesting discussion on the therapy of the activity which has become an absorbing hobby, avocation, or even profession for your profile.

For the Record

If you use a tape recorder, keep it as unobtrusive as possible. People who are not used to being interviewed tend to clam up at the sight of a tape recorder, but you can make them feel comfortable by treating it casually yourself. Always get permission to tape the interview, explaining that it will help you remember the conversation. If someone objects strenuously to being taped, you must defer to your subject's strong wishes. Usually, however, you can melt away any momentary strain the tape recorder causes.

Any time you use your tape recorder, always take notes as well. Tape recorders have been known to go on the blink at the most inopportune times.

As you proceed with your interview, jot down brief descriptive phrases that will recall your subject's physical characteristics. Physical description helps to build character and personality, giving your reader a visual image. We have to see a person physically first before we can identify with that person. Try to catch sensory images as you interview, the tone of your subject's voice; the expression in his or her eyes; mannerisms and gestures, such as a wave of the hand, a tilt to the head, a determined set to the chin.

Such description as, "Anne Taylor's lively conversation and quick steps, as we toured her Victorian house, made it hard for me to believe she'd lived there for more than sixty years," brings the subject alive for your reader. In this one sentence, we get an idea of the subject's age (she's lived in the house for sixty years); her dialogue is lively and her steps quick, which suggest a youthful approach to life.

Other sentences might be: "His deeply tanned face broke into smiles as he spoke of his boyhood days in Missouri."

"Her silvery hair caught the sunlight as she bent to pick one of her prize roses to give me."

"A tall man, he walked with an easy grace as we made our way to the barn to see his collection of antique saddles."

Remember as you interview that you are conducting a guided conversation. You want to keep the conversation focused on the facet of the subject's life that you will use in writing your profile. Incidental material is important in that it adds texture to the portrait, but you can't let the interview wander too far afield for too long.

"As you were saying," is a phrase that gently and politely brings the conversation back to the focal point.

Use phrases appropriate to the situation: "Tell me more about when you broke horses for the Army, started your collection, made your first dollhouse, model airplane, etc."

There are many little ways in which you can bring your subject back from conversational side trips. You'll find such phrases come naturally as you gain experience in interviewing.

Listen for remarks you can use as direct quotes to liven up your profile article. Verify the remark if you aren't sure you took it down correctly. "Did I understand you to say—" is a good way to start the double check.

If your subject says, "Please! Don't use that in your article. I'd die if that got in the paper!" you must find a way to eliminate your subject's objections, or not use the quote.

I always found it helpful to assure the subject I would honor his/her confidence, and go on with the interview. Later, I'd return to the touchy place in the interview. "That was such a wonderful anecdote about your (mother, father, grandfather, or whatever). It makes a great story. Would you really mind if I used it in my article?"

If you've created a warm rapport, many times on second thought your subject will smile and say, "Well, I guess you can."

Or, you can reach a compromise, getting permission to use a part of the story, leaving out perhaps a direct quote from the subject about the incident.

There are always ways to get around touchy situations. Much of your success will depend upon your ability to win your subject's trust and friendship at the beginning of the interview.

If at any time you agree *not* to use material given in confidence during an interview, you must honor your promise. Your reputation as a writer is at stake. Word gets around as to your sincerity and integrity. A writer who honors his word will get referrals.

The Take-Away Bonus

There will come a moment when the conversation reaches a natural conclusion. Your subject is tiring; you're running down. Time to rise, thank your subject for a fine interview, and leave.

There's one important element you should have captured in your interview. As you read through your notes and listen to the tape, keep your inner ear open to catch this element— your subject's emotion and feelings.

As important as it is for your reader to know how something is done or made, or to learn what medical miracles brought about a recovery experience, it is more important for the reader to know how the profile *felt*.

Whether in a photographic study or in a portrait painting, or in a *word* picture, the take-away is in the expression of emotion. When you see that certain light in your profile's eyes followed by a certain tone of voice, mentally tag the emotional response. Capture it and highlight it in your article.

AT THE TYPEWRITER—WHERE TO BEGIN

At last you're set. You're at your typewriter ready to begin to write your profile. Begin where? With your head spinning from all the jottings in your notebook, how do you know where to start?

The answer is quite simple. As with all article writing, begin with your lead. Play around with leads in writing your profiles. You can use an anecdote to kick off your article, some colorful little story your subject related to you during the interview. Or you might start off with a dramatically written account of an exciting situation facing your subject, one that points the way toward what will happen later in the profile.

Another good attention-getting opening is to have your subject speak—the dialogue lead. A startling statement or shocking statistic also gets reader attention in a hurry.

When I was doing my weekly profiles for the paper, I tried

to get my lead set as I drove home from the interview. Something the subject said often gave me the lead. Sometimes it was the poignancy of the situation—as in the recovery type profile. Sometimes it was the colorful personality of the subject that nudged me into a lead.

Of all the writing I've done in my lifetime, none has had greater meaning for me than a profile I wrote called "A Special Person: A Special Love." Love was my key word. The feeling of love was everywhere from the moment I entered my subject's home. The following is how my lead captured this emotion:

> Nowadays everybody talks about love, but nobody does very much about it. Nobody, that is, except people like Mrs. John W. Hagan, who for twenty-one years has been putting into action what love is all about. In more than two decades, she has been mother to some twenty foster children, half of whom are mentally handicapped. Today, there are six of her "babies" in the bright, sun-filled nursery, all of them in need of a special kind of care.

Once you have secured your reader's attention, you're ready for a transition sentence that will carry you into the body of your article. In the *body* of your story profile you set up the little scenes that carry the story forward. It is through the use of complications and small triumphs that you show your subject in action as a living person.

The transition into the body of my article was set with the statement, "From the beginning," Mrs. Hagan said, "this has been a family affair."

In the body, I told how this remarkable woman got interested in being foster mother to children others wouldn't consider because of their mental handicaps. I told how she specifically cared for the children, how they were considered a part of her family, and I described the children as she introduced them to me from their cribs in her nursery. The climax of the profile came with the disclosure that many of the youngsters were Down's Syndrome children, also known as *mongoloid.*

In shaping your ending, circle back to your beginning and

find the key emotion you caught there. Recapture that emotion and build your ending around it. In writing your conclusion, remember the concept of *profile. A study of one facet of a person's life.* Make sure in those final sentences that you've highlighted this element. As in reading a short story, the reader must feel a sense of satisfaction when he comes to the end of your profile. This is the take-away, or the after-glow.

In Mrs. Hagan's story my conclusion circled back to my lead and punched home this theme that had been so clear to me after talking with my subject and seeing her with her foster children.

This is how the piece ended:

> That it takes a very special person to accept the heavy responsibility of caring for mentally handicapped children, Mrs. Hagan doesn't deny.
>
> "It is hard to put into words," she says. "The need is there. You want to do something about it."
>
> She paused a moment to put a toy in a little groping hand. [This action symbolizes my theme of love.]
>
> "Isn't that what everyone is talking about today—love?"

The direct quote, Mrs. Hagan's own words, restates the theme one final time, giving the reader an inspiring take-away.

A poignant photograph of Mrs. Hagan holding one of her "babies" added a nice touch to this memorable profile. When it appeared in the paper the response was tremendous, because people identified with the theme, the great need for love.

PUBLISHING THE PROFILE

There's a wide-open market for profiles in many kinds of magazines and journals, including women's, men's, fraternal, denominational, juvenile, trade, as well as daily newspapers and Sunday supplements.

For every famous person, past or present, there are thousands of people living quiet lives, unknown to all but family and close friends. Among these quiet people are some who will be of special interest to others because of an unusual hobby or activity, or because in their quiet way they contribute to the good of their fellow man. Search them out and write about them. You'll find a satisfaction in beaming the spotlight on someone who deserves attention.

The greatest satisfaction of all will come when your piece is published and readers express the feeling that they enjoyed your article because it told them something new about someone they knew in real life, or someone they knew only from previous writings, or someone they had never known about before.

When you find a special person to write about, as I did with Mrs. Hagan, whatever that special quality is, you'll know why the profile article is one of the most popular in most magazines, and why it's a rewarding kind of writing.

Give profile writing a try. I *know* you'll like it.

CHECKLIST FOR YOUR PROFILE ARTICLES

☑Have you chosen an exciting subject? What did the person do that was exciting and different?

☑What area of your subject's life will you highlight?

☑Have you done your homework—your before-interview research?

☑Do you have a warm-up list of questions prepared?

☑Is your tape recorder in readiness? New batteries? Good tapes?

☑What emotional response did you capture in the interview to *highlight* your word pictures?

The Lord Is
My Shepherd—
Writing the
Inspirational Article

To understand the characteristics and purpose of the inspirational article, you need a clear definition of the word *inspiration* as applied to this type of piece.

Webster's New World Dictionary (my word bible) defines the word *inspiration* as, "Any stimulus to creative thought or action; to cause, guide, communicate, or to motivate by divine influence; as, God inspired the Scriptures."

When choosing a subject for an inspirational article, keep this definition in mind, particularly the phrase, "*Any* stimulus to creative thought or action. . . ." Your stimulus can be *God* if your market is one of the Christian publications. If, however, you're thinking of a nondenominational publication or a publication slanted to a cross-section of readers, you can use such a phrase as, "a Power outside myself," to show the force that motivated a change, or come-to-realize moment.

Readers who are not strongly motivated in a *religious* sense, perhaps having given up church attendance long ago, still seek inspiration, and for this reason, they turn to less religiously oriented (but still inspirational) articles for philosophical help in coping with all kinds of problems.

It's important to target your inspirational writing to a receptive market. Your theme and your style should fit the editorial policy of the publication which in turn mirrors the belief and feelings of the particular readership.

In studying the inspirational market to get a handle on what is acceptable, watch for clues that will give you the right slant. The first clue is often in the titles. "Faith Shines Through" by Shari Smyth, *Guideposts* February '84, is a good example of how the title sets the *inspirational* tone. Other good inspirational titles are "Please Don't Give Up on Me" by Harriet and Terry King, *Reader's Digest,* January '84, "Why Did God Choose Me?" by Charles R. Vess, *Guideposts,* February '84, "I Knew God Was Watching" by Roberta Fletcher, *Guideposts,* April '84.

Make a collection of inspirational titles. Such a list will often give you a theme for *your* article.

The second clue is the so-called *blurb,* that caption written above or below the title. The blurb for "Faith Shines

Through" reads: "But you told me that God was going to take care of them," David whispered. The blurb for "I Knew God Was Watching" is "The long night began for me the moment I entered the kitchen. A night of terror. But all the while . . . I knew God was watching." The blurb for "Why Did God Choose Me?" reads, "People can talk themselves into old age." The author is a seventy-three-year-old man. He rescued someone in a situation requiring great physical strength— "with God's help."

These examples all reflect a *religious* inspirational theme. The authors wrote out of their sincere religious beliefs. Their articles are the expressions of strong Christian faith.

The same type of story could be written effectively without the religious overtones *if* the author showed how his life was changed in some way by some force outside himself. Some writers use words such as, *Fate, Greater Power, Some Unseen Force* to express their conviction that they were helped by something outside themselves.

The third clue can be found in the cover illustrations on inspirational publications, or those using inspirational material. Other clues appear in the flavor and style of the text itself. Some publications like quotes from the Bible used generously throughout an article. Others go lightly. Style depends on editorial policy, a policy that tries hard to meet the tastes and preferences of the readership. Awareness of these differences in expression is essential to a writer's understanding of good marketing practices.

TRIALS AND TRIBULATIONS

Almost any problem you'd write about in a personal experience article, a profile, or a how-to can be written about in an inspirational article. The difference is *the way* in which the problem is solved.

Whereas the resolution of a problem in other types of articles depends mostly on a particular skill, physical stamina, or determination, the problem in inspirational articles is solved through faith in *God, Higher Power, Divine Influence.*

The following examples taken from published inspirational articles will show you how this application of faith and intervention of Divine Influence works. In selecting published articles to help you understand the substance of inspirational writing, I've relied on *Guideposts* and *Reader's Digest* for the most part. *Guideposts* is one of my favorite inspirational publications. Since it is nondenominational, you don't have to worry about understanding a certain doctrine. I've used examples from *Reader's Digest* because many of the inspirational pieces appearing in that magazine are reprints from various religious publications, such as *Christian Science Monitor, Catholic Digest,* and *Christian Life,* to name a few.

Inspirational articles are based on the concept of *negative* against *positive.* A negative abstract, such as fear, is vanquished by a positive, such as love or faith. The positive always wins out over the negative.

The negative situation in the article titled, "I Knew God was Watching" by Roberta Fletcher, *Guideposts,* April '84, begins when the author tells us that she returned home one night at 9:30 to find an intruder in her son's house.

> He was the most awful-looking person: long, dirty blond hair, a black eye, unshaven, in filthy clothes. He stank from sweat and whiskey.

Physical description of a character is one of the fictional techniques borrowed by successful nonfiction writers. The reader experiences the author's fear, thanks to the vivid description. The sight of this evil-looking man sets the problem in motion. Then a second fictional technique is put to use—*dialogue.* When the author enters the kitchen, the intruder snarls, "You sit down and keep quiet!"

"Who are you to tell me what to do in my son's house?" the author demands.

Her son, Robert, lifts his head and in a weak voice pleads, "Mom, please do as he says. I don't want anybody else to be hurt."

This emotion-charged dialogue increases the tension of the situation as straight narration could never do. Since inspirational articles are usually short, approximately 800-1,500 words in length, it is imperative to set up the critical problem and the emotion that accompanies it as quickly as possible. Dialogue is one excellent way to accomplish a strong lead or hook into the article. "I Knew God Was Watching" continues with plenty of dialogue that keeps the tension building as the situation worsens.

After the son's desperate plea for her to keep quiet, the author tells us she trembled in fear, and then she sets the religious tone of the article with the following sentence:

"A strength I know came only from God filled me."

Motivated by strength from God, the author continues in dialogue:

> "Young man," I said, staring into the stranger's bloodshot eyes, "I hope you know what you're doing because we are born-again Christians here and nothing happens in this house that God isn't watching."

This statement reinforces the religious theme. The author continues with more dialogue.

> He (the intruder) glared and barked at me, "Sit down and shut up!" Then he turned to Robert. [Action] "Pull up your shirt and let them see."

The son obeys, pulling up his shirt to reveal that his back is bleeding from many deep stab wounds. The night of terror continues with more violence as the intruder plunges his knife into Robert's back when the son tries to defend himself. [Action.]

Again the author taps the religious theme by telling the reader:

> Then I felt angry again, a *holy* anger, I believe, because I know God doesn't like people to hurt other people. But since I knew He was watching, I tried to stay calm. *I knew God would help us.*

The situation worsens. More violence erupts. The author's daughter-in-law, Bonnie, is told to take off her clothes.

"No!" the author protests.

> [Action:] He swung at me with a knife. "You tie her up."

The author obeys, praying. She is then locked in a closet. (Dark moment)

Now comes the turning point, the intervention of divine influence; where the religious theme is stated even more strongly:

> "Oh Lord," I prayed in the blackness. "Tell us what to do."
>
> Then it was just as if the Lord spoke to me. *Help him get out of the house.*

This is the crisis point. The author beats on the closet door, promising to help the intruder get away. She offers to give him all the money in the house and to drive him anywhere. All the time she's pleading with the intruder, she's praying. She knows, *God will help us.*

We follow the author into the car where she is alone with the intruder. Finally, she gets him out of the car and makes her escape. When she reaches a toll booth, the woman on duty there knows her and calls the police. The police arrive. A call home reveals that Bonnie and the grandchildren are safe. Robert is in the hospital in intensive care with a concussion and a collapsed lung from the stabbing. He will recover.

After this night of terror, the family continues to pray for the intruder. A year later, a young man comes to their door. He brings a letter from the prisoner, the intruder. The letter tells them that the intruder has become a Christian.

The ending gives the reader an inspirational take-away by stating the theme one last time:

> We believed God allowed Jimmy (the intruder) to enter our lives. I think when he was wandering that night looking for a house to rob, he found the right one, in the best meaning of all. And I found out that if the very worst thing I could think of happened to me, *the Lord would be there just as He promised.*

This type of story, the life and death situation, could be slanted to fit markets other than inspirational by stressing other elements, such as ingenuity in outwitting the intruder, skill with a handgun, or any one of many possibilities for turning the tables on the intruder. Roberta Fletcher wrote her article out of her sincere religious convictions. The article is suspenseful, exciting, and inspirational—a wonderful example of a well-written piece slanted carefully to the needs and requirements of a specific market.

Little Things That Mean a Lot

Inspirational articles don't have to be pegged to dramatic life and death struggles. Small, quiet moments of insight and the gaining of new faith can be equally moving.

"Michael's Mouth" by Patricia A. Lorenz (*Guideposts,* February '84) is an example of a completely different type of situation slanted to an inspirational market. The problem in this article revolves around eleven-year-old Michael who had picked up some language on the playground that was "rough around the edges." Michael and his parents have several heart-to-heart talks. Finally, they decide that Michael will write a three-hundred-word essay on "Why God Gave Me a Mouth."

> Michael explains:
>
> God gave us mouths to eat, to sing in church, to whistle while we work, to smile. So dentists wouldn't go broke and lose their jobs. God gave us a mouth so we could say *sorry* when we get in a fight with somebody. God gave us a mouth so we could talk and reason with people before they really get us for it. God gave us a mouth so we could say, "I love my parents!" Love, Michael. P.S. I'm sorry!!!

What reader wouldn't be inspired by this poignant little essay written by an eleven-year-old boy? The author concludes:

> Michael's essay didn't quite capture the reason why we shouldn't use foul language, but it did express many of the rea-

sons we can all be thankful God gave us a mind, a voice, and a heart big enough to say, "I'm sorry." God also gave us a boy named Michael, and for this I'll be eternally grateful.

"Michael's Mouth" proves that inspirational articles can be based upon everyday events in the life of any family.

Faith Can Move Mountains

A third type of inspirational article written by Harriet and Terry King appears in the January '84 issue of *Reader's Digest*, a piece titled, "Please Don't Give Up On Me." This is a different kind of survival situation, a critical physical trauma. The problem is spelled out in the blurb, which reads:

> The comatose teenager was a prisoner in his own body—he could not see, speak, or move, but he knew what was happening around him. How could he escape?

The critical problem seems without solution in the beginning of the article, where we're told that the doctor said the coma could go on for months, years—Bobby may never come out of it. A strong negative.

The beginning also explains how Bobby was hit by a car, sending him flying over the hood, causing critical injury to his brain. We're also told that Bobby wasn't aware of the oncoming car because he was under a crushing burden of guilt. When his stepfather suffered a fatal stroke, he tried to resuscitate him but failed, and so the stepfather died.

"If I'd only known what I was doing, I could have saved Mel" [the stepfather], Bobby thinks.

Now as Bobby lies in a comatose state, a friend of the family sits beside the bed. He'd heard Bobby verbalizing his guilt.

> "You're punishing yourself, aren't you, Bobby?" the friend asks, hoping the boy will hear him, "Don't do it! God loves you [religious theme]. We love you. And we're not going to let you go. But you have to help. Don't let us down, boy. Here, squeeze my hand. You can do it!"

The author gets into Bobby's viewpoint, his mind. Remember, we were told earlier Bobby knew what was happening around him, but couldn't respond.

> Don's voice sounds far away to Bobby, but he hears. He thinks: Don's right. I've got to fight with everything I have. I couldn't save Mel. But somehow I've got to save myself.

This is the turning point. Bobby recovers. The final paragraph again sets the spiritual or religious overtone when, after his recovery and enrollment in a special education program, Bobby says:

> "There's a special strength that can sustain us through almost anything. It comes partly from within, but *even more,* it comes from the *faith* and love of those close to us."

The religious emphasis is not as overt as it was in "God Is Watching," but it's still there, expressed in the words, *faith* and *God,* and in the implication that faith and love can work miracles with God's help.

HOW ARE THE MIGHTY FALLEN

Celebrities in other professions often take time out to share with the reading public the inspirational experiences they've had. I glanced at random through a *Guidepost* collection of such articles and found such well-known names as Mike Douglas and Lawrence Welk. Mike Douglas's article, "When I Needed Watching," is the intimate story of the big brother who taught him how to live. In the article Mike expresses his faith this way:

> In learning to accept and enjoy the blessings at hand, no day since then [referring to the article problem] have I not said my prayers and thanked God for my family and my health and my job.

Lawrence Welk wrote a touching article titled, "The Day the Band Left Me." The blurb in Welk's words explains,

> I felt sick, numb, almost paralyzed with shock . . .

In the article ending, Welk tells us that in his darkest moment when all seemed lost, he went into a church for quiet reflection. He concludes with,

> All men are vulnerable—even Jesus—and whenever we put our love and faith into other human beings, we open ourselves to hurts and disappointments. It's a part of life—we hurt one another—often unintentionally. The only one we can trust completely is God.

Janet Lynn, a bronze medal winner in the 1972 Olympics, wrote an inspirational article titled, "The Lift I Needed." She explains that her dark moment came when she, a star skater, fell—in front of the whole world watching on television. But strangely, she hardly noticed the fall and felt no humiliation or shame.

> I went into my most difficult jump and finished the program well enough to earn the Olympic bronze medal.

She attributes her victory to God being with her. She had wanted to do well not only for her own personal satisfaction but as an expression of her gratitude for the talent and skill she felt God had given her. Her last statement reads,

> For in completely giving ourselves to Him, He gives us back the best part of ourselves so we can face whatever life brings us.

Janet Lynn wrote her own story, but there's always a demand for so-called ghost writers, who write a celebrity's story for him or her. Not all gifted and accomplished people in fields other than writing can author their own story. Even if they can write, many celebrities haven't the time to sit down day after day at a typewriter or word processor. That's where you step into the picture.

Watch your newspaper for the names of celebrities who are coming to your area to give a talk on some inspirational experience they've had. Plan to attend the lecture. There are often ways you can meet the celebrity or set up an appointment for an interview: through the help of the organization that sponsors the talk, through the public relations firm representing the celebrity, or by writing directly to the person.

A firm called *Celebrity Service, Inc.,* 171 W. 57th St., New York, NY 10019, will send you addresses of celebrities for $10.

THE PATTERN

Whether inspirational articles you read were by an unknown, by a celebrity, or by a professional writer, you'll find that certain basic elements appear over and over:

1. Simplicity of style, a way of writing that makes readers feel they are with the writer, sharing the experience.

2. An honest and open confession of the writer's low moment in which any one of the negatives—fear, doubt, loss of faith—overwhelmed him or her.

3. Dramatization: action and dialogue, as well as good characterization, conflict, and suspense.

4. An exciting climax that *shows* the reader why and how the writer felt the influence of a greater Power.

5. A statement of faith in this outer force, whether referred to as God, Divine Power, Fate, or some other term meaningful to the writer, a faith that brought about the turning point in the author's life. Inspirational writing isn't difficult to learn if you keep these five points in mind. Copy them into your notebook for quick reference as you write.

With the exception of the strong expression of faith in the inspirational piece, the other basic elements—style, dramatization, openness, and so forth—are found also in the personal experience article. It's understandable that these two types are very much alike in many ways, because an inspirational article is a *kind* of personal experience. If you have success writing one, you'll most likely find the other easy to write. Both kinds are popular in a variety of markets.

One word of warning: Not everyone can write inspirational articles. As in any type of writing, you must believe in the stories you put on paper. If you think inspirational articles are too sentimental, too "square," too everything you're not, the category isn't for you. You'll have better luck with one of the other article types discussed in this book.

But before you turn your back on this type of writing, at least read and consider a few inspirational articles condensed in *Reader's Digest.* You might be surprised to hear yourself say, "I could have written that!" There's a good chance you could—once your interest is captured. You are free to express your concept of spiritual inspiration in *your* terms.

HOW TO DO IT

The purpose of inspirational articles is to help the reader in some way through sharing an experience. With few exceptions, use first-person viewpoint (use *I* and *we* in telling your story). Third-person viewpoint—he, she, or the name of some other person—would be used only in rare situations where you were close to or shared in someone else's inspirational experience.

Start with the negative and work through to the positive. Open with a scene showing yourself (or whomever you're writing about) facing a critical problem—any situation that forces a win-or-lose resolution. The critical problem can be a threat to life as reflected in "God is Watching" and in "Don't Give Up on Me," or it can evolve out of a familiar family situation, as seen in "Michael's Mouth."

The critical problem situation will show you, or someone else, with a *negative* attitude which prevents the resolution of the problem. The negative attitude was terror in "God is

Watching," despair in "Don't Give Up on Me," and worry in "Michael's Mouth."

Reach for the universal by tapping the basic human emotions: love, fear, grief, loneliness, hope, faith—feelings we all have at one time or another.

Be open in your writing. Share your feelings, whether negative or positive, with readers. Confide in them, letting them see your weaknesses in your hour of trial.

Plan your *climax* scene, the scene in which the negative will change to a positive. What causes the change in attitude? It must be an event, something strong enough to force the change in thinking. The climax must escalate the problem to the breaking point. Then you, the narrator, or the character you're writing about, turn to a Higher Power for help.

Use anecdote to *dramatize* your inspirational experience. *Show* the reader how prayer, silent or aloud, and your belief in a Power greater than yourself, helped you turn your life around by changing your attitude, or by giving you courage and strength when you needed it most.

Make sure your article has a take-away, something readers can apply to their own lives. Make your readers feel that they, too, can turn their lives around by faith in "divine influence," however they interpret the concept.

WHERE TO FIND IT

As in selecting material for personal experience articles, the best source to use in writing inspirational articles is your own life. You saw from the examples I gave you in this chapter how different writers drew upon the traumas in their own lives to give the inspiration to others.

The teachings of *all* religions provide us with inspirational material that we as writers can use to help the reader solve problems. And the Bible is an unending source of themes and problems you can use in your inspirational articles. The way we live may change, but human emotions stay the same. In Biblical times, people were torn with jealousy, were shattered

by grief at the loss of a loved one, and they had their faith tested—all the emotions we feel today as we face similar problems. It's important to remind your reader that the same emotions and needs exist today when you use a reference to a Biblical event or a Scripture quote. Make the connection between
the *then* and the *now.*

People close to you are another source. Because certain
people *are* so close to us, we feel their pain as our own. Perhaps you've helped friends through some crisis. You *know*
what it is that saved them. If you can find the *Divine Influence*
in any of these experiences, those that happen to you and
those that overtake your family and friends, you have subject
matter for an inspirational article.

You can write inspirational articles using the lives of people you may not know intimately. But it is harder, I feel, to capture that special essence, that warm, caring style of expression
that is so important to inspirational writing.

WHERE TO SELL IT

There are many inspirational and religious markets open to
you if you decide to try this type of article. Many of our most
successful writers got their start writing for denominational
publications—writers such as Norman Vincent Peale, Marjo-
rie Holmes, Ardis Whitman, Helen Hayes, Taylor Caldwell,
Jean Stapleton, and many, many more. You've probably seen
inspirational articles by these writers, not only in religious
publications, but in magazines slanted toward women, the
family, and members of fraternal organizations.

Faith can be expressed in many different ways, depending
on the readership and the market. Readers looking for spiritual
inspiration and guidance tend to stick with the publications of
their own denomination. A Catholic feels comfortable reading
any one of the magazines published by the Catholic press. *The
Lutheran, The Episcopalian,* the *Presbyterian Survey,* the
United Methodist Reporter, and the *Baptist Herald* are a few
other examples of denominational publications. You don't

have to be of the same religious faith in order to write for a denominational publication, but you must respect your readers' beliefs—whatever their religious convictions may be. Check to make sure you've used the correct terminology when referring to the symbols and rituals of a particular faith.

You'll find a complete list of religious publications published in the December issues of both *The Writer* and *Writer's Digest. Writer's Market* lists a complete compilation of all kinds of markets, and devotes more than thirty pages to names and addresses of various religious publishers.

Most denominational publications will send you their editorial guidesheets if you send a self-addressed, stamped envelope. By studying the guidesheets you'll have a clear picture of what a specific editor wants in the way of subject matter and presentation.

In the beginning, the pay is often low—starting at 4¢ a word. Hardly a proper financial remuneration for hours at the typewriter. There is always the chance, however, that something you write will have such an impact on the readership of a denominational publication that it will attract the editorial eye at *Reader's Digest.* And many times an inspirational article will be picked up by other religious magazines as a reprint with an additional monetary reward for you.

Sometimes just a few minor changes in your manuscript will bring it in line with the particular slant of the reprint publication. Many writers I know boast that they have sold a certain inspirational article up to twenty times.

Other Rewards

While it is important to be paid in cold cash for the fruits of your labor, it is equally important to feel that inner glow that comes from knowing what you wrote helped someone in some way—if only for a moment.

The best writing transcends time and geographical distance. If you decide to write inspirational articles and you're good enough to publish, you'll find a readership warmly appreciative of the help your articles bring. Readers will write letters to you and to your editors expressing gratitude because you shared a very special moment in your life, the moment when you found a faith you thought you'd lost.

What greater reward could there be than to know that you helped someone through his or her darkest hour, and *inspired* someone to a rebirth of faith that will in some way provide the turning point—a second chance.

That, in essence, is what the inspirational article accomplishes, and that is why it remains one of the most popular types, the kind found in just about every category of magazine.

CHECKLIST FOR YOUR INSPIRATIONAL ARTICLES

☑Did you stick to one problem? One theme?

☑Is your style of writing inspirational? Have you drawn upon motivational quotations from the Bible, poetry, or other sources to give a firm basis for your theme?

☑Does your article reflect your sincerity? Does it prove to the reader that you *believe* what you wrote?

☑Have you avoided a preachy tone?

☑Did you take the time to familiarize yourself with the doctrines and symbols of a particular faith?

☑Does your article have a strong take-away for the reader in terms of a *spiritual* point of view? Do you show the power of faith and prayer through numerous anecdotes of how other people (as well as yourself) solved their problems with the help of *Divine Influence?*

When the
Writer Teaches—
Writing the
How-to Article

The how-to is one of the most popular types of articles published in today's newspapers and magazines. If you can write articles telling others how you found an easier or faster way to build or make something, or how you found a new solution to an old problem (or a new one), you'll find a wide open market waiting for you.

In addition to the popularity of how-to-make and -do articles and problem-solving ones, there's a big market for the self-improvement type of how-tos, pieces in which you show how you learned new habits to replace bad ones; how you developed a new skill, or how you made yourself into a more attractive and lovable person.

Why are how-to articles so in demand? There are many answers to this question. Strangely enough, in our mechanized world where almost everything comes to us through the push of a button or the turn of a dial, where the only struggle in cooking is often the opening of the well-sealed frozen package, there is a great hunger felt by many people, the young included, to go back to basics and to the "old" way of doing things. People want to know how to start from scratch. The almost forgotten art of quilt making is once again popular. Many other almost lost skills such as knitting, tatting, weaving, macrame, furniture making (Jimmy Carter and his chairs), and a host of other *handwork* activities are now included in school curriculums and in adult education programs.

The upsurge in do-it-yourself projects is not only a reflection of an interest in the nostalgic past, however. It is a result of our change in lifestyle. More people are living longer in good health with more time to do the things they've always dreamed of doing. Freed from time-consuming tasks, thanks to modern conveniences, people of all ages have more time to take up hobbies and to learn new skills.

Not everyone can get to a class; those who can't, pick up newspapers and magazines to keep informed and to read over and over again *how to make, how to build, and how to be.*

Glance at the Table of Contents page of almost any magazine and you'll see the word *how-to.* You'll find it helpful in your study of the how-to article to keep a list of titles with the word *how-to* included. *How-to* is one of the most salable word signals in print today. You can capitalize on its salability by making a list of your own skills and accomplishments for use as material for your how-to articles.

SUCCESS STORIES

Many of my students made their first sales by writing various kinds of how-to articles. One student, Charles Floyd, missed a class because he was reroofing his house *himself.*

"Write an article about it, Charles," I told him. "Bring it to class next week."

The next week Charles returned with article in hand, a big smile lighting his face. He told the class how he'd put his wife up on the roof to photograph his roofing procedure step by step. Eventually the article sold to *Popular Mechanics.*

Charles sold a second how-to on a space-saver bookcase he built, and a third on how he invented a traveling light to put over his garage workbench. Each article was accompanied by black-and-white photographs showing exactly how he accomplished his goal. The second and third articles also sold to *Popular Mechanics.* Another beginning writer was on his way.

Gerry Fleming was another student who began her writing career with how-tos. Gerry's absorbing interest was in the American West and in treasure hunting. I couldn't begin to list her sales in the allowed space. I can only mention a few, such as her articles titled, "How to Buy a Metal Detector," "How to Treasure Hunt Safely in Off-the-Beaten-Path Places," and many other "camping" pieces.

Gerry hit the jackpot with her how-to technique when she finally wrote what she knew about keeping Cub Scouts busy. As a den mother, she was appalled to find that there was virtually nothing published to help den mothers plan craft and building projects to occupy their active Cub Scouts during meetings. Gerry wrote a book on the subject, "Scrapcrafts for Youth Groups."

Still another student, Diane Crawford, recently achieved

publication with her articles on what she calls "Handy Hints," how-tos on sewing and various other handwork that she likes to do in her spare time. Her interest in charitable organizations led to a how-to sale, "The Box Project," to *Lady's Circle.*

"I've sold a total of twenty how-to articles," Diane told me at our last class meeting. "I sell to markets such as *Junior Trails, Woman's World, Grit, California Highway Patrolman, Family Circle, Touch, Crafts, Byline,* and *Refunder's Magazine.*"

Diane is a firm believer in the rule of *write what you know.* She took a good look at what she had to offer in the way of interesting skills and ideas, then started writing how-tos.

Bernice Curler, another successful writer in the how-to category, confesses she's a collector.

> Every nook and cranny of my house proves it. One of my collections is made up of old cookbooks. The first how-to I ever sold was to a little magazine called *The Nebraska Electric Farmer.* In the article, I told how to have fun browsing through old cookbooks. The article came out under the title, "Grandma was a Blue Ribbon Cook." Using different anecdotes and different recipes, I sold the same idea to *Modern Maturity* with the title, "Treasure Hunting Through Old Cook Books."
>
> After these two article sales, I wrote and sold many more on anything that interested and excited me. I sold "Make a Mushroom Candle" to *American Girl,* and "Five Cogs in the Wheel of Success," on how to stimulate self-drive, to *Success Unlimited.* This article was picked up as a reprint by the Amway Company for an article in their sales training manual.

Bernice has this advice for beginners.

> Know your market. If you know the readership, you can write several articles out of the same source material by changing the slant and using a different type of lead.
>
> For instance, from my brother-in-law, an artist, I learned how to use imitation gold leaf to gild picture frames inexpensively. I sold a how-to article on this subject to *Canadian Homes,* titled "The Midas Touch." By taking a different approach for different

readerships directed to a middle-income, higher income, and home-interested reader, I used the same basic information for another article, titled "Secret of Framing," which sold to *House Beautiful.*

Still another sale on the same subject of framing a picture sold to *Lady's Circle,* a family-oriented magazine. My lead was: "A picture that's a first-place winner should be framed in gold." I went on to tell how I hunted for the proper but inexpensive frame and finally decided to make my own. The title on the published article in *Lady's Circle* was "How To Make an Elegant Imitation Gold Leaf Frame."

There are several ways in which you can use the same how-to idea for several noncompetitive markets. As I mentioned, you can change the lead by using one type for one article and another type for a second, third, and so on. If you've forgotten the different types of leads, review the discussion of leads in Chapter 1.

Bernice's sales are a good example of how a writer can take one article idea and spin it off into several sales. The key to multiple sales from one idea is in Bernice's explanation that she changed the slant and used different leads for each article sale. She took "different approaches," one article slanted to middle-income readers, another to home-interested ones, and another to a higher income readership.

In spinning off your article ideas, make sure that you submit to noncompetitive markets. Bernice knew that *Canadian Homes* magazine drew a different readership from that of *House Beautiful* with its mostly American readership.

SECRETS OF SUCCESS

The students I told you about, students who are examples of how the beginner can get published through the how-to, all share common requisites for success:

1. Taking the time to learn the basic techniques for writing salable nonfiction, the same techniques presented to you in this book.

2. Writing about what they can do well.

3. Getting excited about what they do and making this excitement shine through in their writing.

4. Making a list of possible markets, markets they had researched *before* they mailed.

5. Not giving up when they got rejections but continuing to submit material.

6. While heeding the requirements for a specific market, they were able to inject freshness and style into their writing.

TYPES OF HOW-TOS

There are many kinds of how-to articles you can write in addition to the *how to make and do* kind. The students' examples I've shown you I think of as the *physical* or concrete kind of how-to, inasmuch as they require two hands and some sort of material: wood, cloth, paint, nails, potting soil, seeds, etc.

Another type of how-to is one I tag *psychological.* There *can be* concrete material involved as in an article showing one how to improve one's taste in dress, or in a piece describing how the use of certain skin care products can lead to a better complexion and a more attractive makeup which in turn can lead to a better self-image. The main focus in this type of how-to, however, is on the *psychological* benefits rather than on the products used. The material objects involved are secondary—necessary, but not the primary interest. The primary interest is in attaining a psychological lift. We call this type of how-to, the *self-help* piece.

As is true of other easy-to-write and -sell kinds of articles discussed in this book, if you're interested in learning the required technique, it won't take you long to grasp the writing technique that goes into *all* how-to articles.

Keep in mind that you are not only a writer when you put together a how-to article; you're also a teacher. You don't have the advantage of a classroom situation, however. When a question arises, there are no hands going up to tell you that you didn't make some point quite clear. There's only the unseen reader somewhere staring down at the words you wrote, brow furrowed in a puzzled frown. You only get *one* chance to make yourself understood.

HOW-TO-DO HOW-TOS

In the first type of how-to, you show the reader how to make or create products, such as hand-knit garments, custom-designed jewelry, cuddly toys, or a more convenient workbench. You may tell how to convert wasted attic space into additional bedrooms or a playroom, or how to do it yourself in just about any area you can think of.

This type of article can also focus on how to *make do.* As an example of making do, my brother-in-law, Gordon, recently made a fine wood shed out of lumber taken from an old abandoned corn crib. The corn crib had fallen in, but the lumber was still good.

> "That corn crib must have been almost a hundred years old," my brother-in-law told me, as I admired his latest project. "The shingles were pretty moldy, but I cleaned them off, turned them over and they made a good sound roof for the new shed."

I recognized a good possibility for a *make-do* how-to. Any time you can show someone how to take material he already has on hand to make something new, you've added a real plus to your do-it-yourself how-to article.

When writing how-to do articles, you must present your instructions in clear, easy-to-understand language. Check and double-check your measurements, the amount of material needed to complete the project, whether your article shows how to build a birdbath, make a quilt, knit a baby sweater, or convert a corn crib into a woodshed.

Here are several important guidelines to success in writing salable how-to articles.

1. Tell the reader where to get the material, how much to

get, and the approximate cost.

Always tailor the cost of your do-it-yourself project to the reader's purse. There's no use in trying to sell a how-to article on building an expensive lanai on a beachfront home to a publication read by people struggling to make ends meet in a city apartment complex.

2. Be specific. It isn't enough to tell the reader that something doesn't cost much. Prices vary across the country, but you can estimate the cost in round figures, such as "under five or ten dollars"; "not more than fifty dollars," etc.

In addition to wanting to know the cost, readers want to know how long it takes to build or make something. Tell your readers how much time they should expect to invest in the project.

3. Keep your instructions as simple as possible. You achieve simplicity by using short sentences and paragraphs limited to one facet of instruction. Avoid giving too many ideas in a lump. Break your explanations down into easy-to-digest segments.

4. Step-by-step illustrations or photographs are a great help to the reader in visualizing your instructions. Show the crafting of a product from the ground up—first you do this, and then you do that, following through in easy-to-comprehend guidelines.

If you don't know much about photography, by all means take a course in the subject. Or you might have a friend who is a good photographer. He or she might be more than happy to give you instruction for free or for a nominal fee; or you might work out an agreement where your friend takes the pictures and you do the writing.

Your photographs must look professional—clear, sharp pictures that illustrate the procedure you use in a craft or construction article step-by-step.

Unless you are a professional artist with sales to your credit, don't try to sketch or draw your own illustrations. Again, find someone to work with you, someone whose work is of professional quality.

5. Finally, make sure you've included in your article the joy,

the satisfaction, and the sense of accomplishment that comes to you through the making or building of your hand-crafted product.

What to Write About

Here are just a few ideas for how-to-make and -do articles:

Construction—build your own doghouse, dollhouse, darkroom, workroom, woodshed, gameroom, bookcase, desk, model planes and ships, cabin, house, boat, furniture.

Cooking—everything from gingerbread men to a full-course menu.

Domestic—how to clean house properly. How to avoid and get rid of clutter. How to accident-proof your kitchen, bathroom, pool area. How to take care of your possessions, furniture, silver, rugs, linens.

Gardening—how to plant and grow every conceivable kind of vegetable, flower, and herb. How to get rid of insect pests.

Handcraft—knitting, quilting, sewing, needlepoint, crocheting, macramé, weaving, ceramics, batik, decoupage.

HELP YOURSELF TO SELF-HELP

The *self-help* how-to article focuses on how-to-*be*. In this kind of how-to, you work hard to motivate a change in attitudes which in turn brings about a happier state of mind. These articles may deal with the same problems as those in inspirational articles, problems such as coping with loss of a loved one, loneliness, fear—any negative emotion brought on by a difficult situation. The difference between the how-to and the inspirational article is in the *solution to the problem.*

In the inspiration type of article, the solution to the problem comes about through faith in the power of *Divine Influence* to point the way at the critical hour. In self-help articles, the solution comes through recognizing one's own innate strength of character and allowing it to assert itself when needed most. The writer says, in effect, "You can overcome,

cope, manage, survive—if you will follow my suggestions."
The writer then offers concrete steps the reader must follow
in order to change a negative attitude into a positive one. The
phrase, *self-help* spells the premise of this kind of article. You
get there, or you win, by *helping yourself.*

Self-help how-tos require a very special approach to a
subject. You must have a wealth of solid information, backed
up by careful research. Often you must document your methods and theories with the expertise and experiences of others
involved with the subject you're writing about.

How Can I Help?

The structure of these articles is clear cut:

1. Start with the problem clearly stated.
2. Talk about possible causes of the problem.
3. Give five or six easy-to-follow suggestions for solving the
   problem.

Here's how we might structure the self-help article on retirement.

1. *The lead. The problem clearly stated:*

For thirty years you've had the house to yourself except
for the children clattering through the kitchen. Suddenly,
you're no longer Queen of all you survey. You've got a King on
the throne—your husband has retired! He's underfoot twenty-
four hours a day. Not only is he under your feet, he's constantly
telling you how to do what you've been doing for more years
than you wish to recall.

You feel as if you're in a cage.

2. *Causes of problem—the motivation for problem.*

You feel sorry for that man of yours wandering like a lost
soul through your kitchen, living room, and yard. You realize
retirement isn't the dream he visualized. It's turning into a
nightmare because he didn't retire *to* something. He's got too
many idle hours unfilled.

3. *Five or six suggestions to cure problem.*

Is there a solution? Of course there is. Start off by making your husband your partner instead of a hindrance. Let him share in a few of your activities. Don't lock him out.

Encourage him to talk about what he'd like to do and then give him the support he needs.

You can think of two or three other ways this problem could be solved. Write them down. Finish the article.

Brainstorming the Theme

Here are several self-help article ideas:

Alcoholism—How to treat it.

Drug Abuse—How to get help.

Health—How to lose or gain weight. How to deal with debilitating illness in yourself or a loved one. How to have healthier skin, hair, eyes, heart, lungs, etc.

Housing—How to buy and how to sell your home and other real estate. How to cope with the empty-nest blues. How to co-exist with grown children who return to the nest. How to survive a move.

Love—How to find it. How to keep it. How to survive losing it.

Money—How to get it. How to invest it. How to cope with losing it.

Career—How to get a job. How to keep a job. How to advance your career. How to survive when you lose your job.

Personal Development—How to overcome shyness, loneliness, fear, grief, poor self-image, insecurity.

Relationships—How to get along better with spouses, children, parents, friends, bosses, fellow employees.

Retirement—How to make the adjustment to having a spouse home all day. How to shift gears into other activities. How to choose the right retirement location.

INFORMATION PLEASE

The third kind of how-to article informs the reader on a particular subject or situation, rather than describing how to use a skill to build, to make, or to make do.

Subjects to write on under this category might be:

Shopping—How to get the best bargains in anything. Clothes. Furniture. Produce. Meat. Canned goods. Automobiles. Homes. Loans. Travel Clubs.

Services—How to get a good doctor, lawyer, dentist, accountant, psychiatrist, teacher, class, home repair, loan, travel bureau.

For information on a given subject, as in writing other types of how-tos and other types of articles, you can draw on your own experience. It is wise, however, to back up your own experience with information researched from experts in a particular field, as for instance, travel, services, and shopping. Writing off the top of your head isn't enough. Editors want *your* ideas, supported by the opinions and expertise of authorities.

Go to the professional source: your doctor, lawyer, dentist, accountant. Tell your physician you're doing an article on how to find a good doctor when you're a stranger in town—or any other topic you choose. You'll be surprised at how eager the experts are to share what they know with a writer. That old magic of seeing one's name in print is working for you. Your authority will be pleased and proud when he sees his advice published in your article.

WHICH HOW-TO SHOULD YOU WRITE?

Inventory your own skills, hobbies, experiences, and jot down the items that have a special interest or meaning in your life. What do you like to do best in your spare time? Would other people find the same enjoyment if they were to follow your lead? Is what you do inexpensive and are the materials readily available? Is it rewarding and fun?

If you've coped successfully in a difficult life situation, how did you do it?

Whatever type of how-to you write, be positive in your own attitude toward the project, the situation, or the condition. Let your enthusiasm and feeling of excitement breathe life into your article.

The lead for a how-to article is easy to write. Its purpose is to give instant reader identification with the subject of the how-to, whether it's something involving making, building, growing, or self-help.

As an illustration of the simplicity of a how-to lead, here are a few examples from magazines.

Title: "Tie One On!" in which the reader is told how to "Whip up witty Christmas aprons for kitchen helpers" (blurb).

Lead: "Dad's fireplace apron, Mom's candle apron, and the child's tree apron (all illustrated in color on the facing page) are take-offs on the butcher-block apron style."

See how simple that lead is? We know instantly we're going to learn to make aprons. The article appears in the December 11 '84, issue of *Woman's World*, and is written by Ruth Philips.

The instructions follow the lead in an orderly fashion. "First you back all fabric pieces." A step-by-step procedure is given for each type of apron, as well as material needed and exact dimensions.

In the section titled "Medinews" in the *Ladies' Home Journal*, May '84, is a short (under 300 words) filler-type how-to titled, "Mastering Motion Sickness." The page is staff written by Beth Weinhouse.

The lead: "For many people, travel—whether by car, bus, train, plane or boat—means motion sickness. But NASA physician and engineer Dr. Bryant Crammer . . . has found that there are psychological factors that contribute to queasiness."

Again the instructions to avoid the psychological conditions that lead to motion sickness are given in a simple and straightforward manner, beginning with a suggestion that the reader try other methods before resorting to medication, methods such as breathing slowly and deeply with mouth open, and concentrating on tensing and relaxing the body.

In a self-help type of how-to titled "Put P.E.P. into Your Life," by Robert L. Gedaliah (*Reader's Digest,* October '84, article condensed from *P.E.P.—The Productivity Effectiveness Program,* a paperback published by Holt, Rinehart and Winston), the lead is simple, a direct address type wherein the author starts off with:

> It's 2 P.M., but you feel as though you've already put in a full day. Work is piling up on your desk. The phone is ringing, etc.

What reader wouldn't identify with that stressful state in today's world? The premise of the article follows the *you* lead: "The truth is, you're not really exhausted. But your inability to deal with stress has made you feel that way."

The author then tells us how to avoid this stressful feeling in seven easy-to-follow suggestions.

I repeat: Whatever kind of how-to you choose to write, remember to keep your lead simple and direct. Focus it on the specific subject.

If you've never written any type of how-to article before, it's a good idea to begin with *short* articles—these run from 500 words to approximately 1500. Get started by making a collection of the kinds of articles you particularly like. Clip examples and enter the title, the author, the name of the publication, and the date of publication in your notebook or on index cards. Tag the article as to the specific type of how-to it is. Identify the kind of lead. Did the article begin with a quotation, an anecdote, a description, or with dialogue? How many step-by-step instructions were given, if the article was a build-it or make-it type? How many suggestions were given if the article was focused on changing attitudes in a self-help how-to?

How-to articles meet the same competition as other types of articles. You may think you're the only one building a doghouse with solar heating, but at the same time you get your inspiration, so do a lot of other people. It's always a good idea to query an editor before you submit.

You'll find many markets for your how-to articles in *Writer's Market* and *The Writer's Handbook,* as well as in various monthly issues of *The Writer* and *Writer's Digest.*

Readers' Guide to Periodical Literature is a library reference book that will tell you what other articles have been written on your subject. Knowing that, you have a better chance to give your piece a fresh slant or treatment.

THE PAYOFF

There is no joy quite like that which comes when you share what you know, what you've learned, and what you've experienced with someone else. If you're enthusiastic and excited about an idea or a project, and you reflect your feelings in writing your how-to articles, you'll have grateful and appreciative readers who will write you letters thanking you for getting them started.

In addition, you'll build up publication credits and receive checks for your articles. To begin with, the pay may not be as high as in some other kinds of writing, but how-to article writing has paid off for many professional writers in a nice steady income. These articles can be written relatively quickly once you master the simple techniques I've given you in this chapter. Therefore, the small checks from many sales add up.

I've been writing how-to articles for many years, my pieces appearing in *Writer's Digest* and various other publications. I've loved every moment of it, and so will you if you decide to try this ever-popular category of nonfiction.

CHECKLIST FOR YOUR HOW-TO ARTICLES

☑What specific how-to did you write?
    How to Make and Do
    self-help—How to Cope
    Informational—How to Get the Best

☑If your article tells how to make or how to do, are your instructions easy to follow in a step-by-step sequence? If it's a self-help article, did you offer concrete suggestions for changing the negative to positive?

☑Did you double-check your facts and figures, your quotations, and your anecdotes? (Anecdotes must prove a point; tag each one as to the point it proves.)

☑Do you have plenty of backup from other people who have succeeded in making the product you're writing about, or who have successfully handled a similar self-help situation?

☑Have you put a shine to your article through expression of your own positive attitude, your enthusiasm, your excitement, and your strong conviction that the reader will experience the same emotions through following your instructions?

Those Were the
Days—
Writing the
Nostalgia Article

Memory was given mortals so they could have roses in December.

Anonymous

These words best express the importance memory plays in human experience. No matter how young or how old we are, there are times when we need to breathe the fragrance of yesterday's roses, and to feel the warmth of sunny days past.

You don't have to be Grandma or Grandpa Moses to write about the good old days. With the world changing so fast, the new becomes old almost overnight. Many people feel a sense of panic. They wonder how they'll keep up with it all, and they often long for the old way of doing things. It's quite a shock to go to work one morning and find your familiar and trusty typewriter replaced with a computer, the workings of which you'll be expected to learn—in a hurry.

It's even more shocking for some of us to realize that the forties and fifties are now ancient history to the younger generation, and that even the seventies are becoming the shadowed past as we move closer to the nineties and the turn of the century.

As we all become busier and busier, time seems to whiz by at an alarming rate. There's so little of it left to enjoy the traditional rituals that were once a part of our daily lives. We long for the leisurely pace of yesterday.

The need to look back over our shoulders at days gone by is one of the reasons nostalgia articles appear frequently in many magazines and in various newspaper Sunday supplement sections. In reading about the past, we relive what now seem like "the good old days." An article with a nostalgic tone appeals to older readers because it allows them to vicariously savor the days of their youth again. Nostalgia pieces also provide a learning experience for those too young to have much of a past to remember. Young people want to know what the world was like when their parents were *their* age, and people in their thirties and forties begin to think nostalgically of their own childhood and adolescent days.

If you're the kind of writer who has a genuine feeling for the past, if you can give the reader "roses in December," you'll find a good market for your articles.

IT SEEMS LIKE ONLY YESTERDAY . . .

To have a feeling for the past means that you're something of a sentimentalist. Your eyes grow misty as you think of childhood Christmases when you tiptoed down the stairs to see what Santa had brought. What wouldn't you give to be at that dining room table groaning with the weight of the turkey, and to listen to the buzz of good conversation from all the uncles, aunts, grandparents, brothers, and sisters gathered together.

Some of those loved ones may be gone now, but as you think of them, and as you write about them, they come alive. Your readers will find memories stirring in their minds and hearts when they read your article about your Christmas in "the good old days."

A delightful Christmas reminiscence appeared in a piece called "Mother's Day," written by Dwight Chapin, a regular columnist for the *San Francisco Examiner.*

Chapin sets the nostalgic mood with this lead:

> The smells were of turkey roasting slowly, of pumpkin pies cooling on a wire rack, of brown sugar and butter melting on sweet potatoes.

One of the best ways to recapture the past is through the sense of smell. A fragrance, a mouth-watering cooking odor can bring the past back vividly. Chapin makes good use of this device in his opening.

The author then sets the premise of his article—the theme that will give the reader the take-away at the end.

> My mother loved Christmas more than anyone I've ever known. That was probably because she was the most giving person I've ever known.

Giving—a perfect theme for a nostalgic Christmas piece.

The article shows the family going through the traditions of the time: his mother's Christmas shopping and attempts to hide the gifts; the careful selection of the tree and the decorating; the tags that read "From Santa."

The ending circles back to the opening theme and leaves us with a warm glow as we, the readers, recall our own childhood Christmases.

> She's been gone for several years now, but I still remember her at Christmas. Her rituals. Her joy. Her standing at the kitchen sink, hands shriveled by the hot soapy water, so content because she was doing what she had always done and what she wanted to do.
>
> I used to wonder what made her the way she was, but I don't anymore. In reverence, I just accept.

I think you'll agree that this little nostalgia piece is moving in its simplicity of style and in the sincerity of the author's emotions—feelings of affection and gratitude with which we identify because of our own treasured memories of our mothers and Christmases past.

Many other writers have written hundreds of Christmas pieces in the same vein as Chapin's "Mother's Day." Magazines, newspapers, and books will continue to carry such stories year after year because they give us a chance to relive the good old days once more.

DO YOU REMEMBER WHEN?

We've already discussed the importance of selecting subjects of universal interest in writing other types of articles. Universality is equally important in writing nostalgia.

To refresh your memory, a universal subject is one that has great interest to a large number of people. Whatever type of article you write, including nostalgia, your choice of a universal subject is another way for you to reach your reader. What has tender, nostalgic meaning for you must also arouse the same emotions in the reader.

Universal subjects include:

Childhood memories—Birthday parties. The Tooth Fairy. New baby brother or sister. First visit to the doctor or hospital. (In a nostalgia article, traumas in the past are handled with humor and gentleness.) Favorite games. First day at school. Moving to a new house. Visits to grandparents. Special occasions, such as Christmas, Fourth of July picnics, summer vacations.

Adolescence—Entering high school and college. First boy-friend/girlfriend. First date. First love. Favorite movies, radio shows, or television programs.

Sports events, such as your first away-from-home game. Your first Olympics. Winning the state championship.

Historical events, such as the day the President came to your city or town—whoever he was when you were young. The first time you saw a rocket blast off for outer space.

Marriage and early days following—The wedding day. First home. First baby. Your child's first day at school. First Christmas in your own home. Your first vacation as an adult.

First job—Clerking in a department store. Your first office job. The summer you worked on a ranch or dairy farm. You might have been very young and got your first job in a Mom and Pop neighborhood grocery store as bagger or carry-out person.

This is only a *partial* list of subjects that have universal appeal, meaning that in some way we've all experienced these events, or ones very similar. To have universal appeal doesn't mean that all readers experienced what you did in exactly the same way, but there must be something in your memory of this past event that triggers a similar memory for the reader.

When the reader smiles and thinks, "That reminds me of the day when I. . . ." or, "The old man in that article was just like my Grandpa"—you've made the connection.

BEYOND TIME AND PLACE

The time span between the present and the past is not the most important element in writing about the good old days. What counts is being able to make the connection between the *then* and the *now,* however long the bridge of time. For the reader of any age to identify with your nostalgic recollections, you must establish a strong link between the present and the past. By making reference to something in the present, which is like—or not like—the way it was in the good old days, you give your reader a handle to grab.

As an example, you might be writing how it was when you had to trudge through knee-deep snow to get to school. Young people today hop on buses and sometimes travel miles to get to their designated school. You could make the connection between the then and now by asking the question: Are things better today? Is it any easier to get up early, stand in the cold waiting for a school bus, riding it through congested traffic, than it was to run out your door, meet with a pal, and hurry off to school on Shank's Mare—your own two feet? You could then build up a picture of that walk to school: the snowballs, the clean unpolluted air, and the peace and quiet of a country lane.

You could take the other view, pointing out how lucky kids today are, warm and snug in their bus seats and delivered usually up to the front door at school. The connection is made through the mode of transportation and the image of going off to school—something with which we all identify.

If you can find the connection between the then and now, you have stronger reader identification than if you write solely about how things were in the past and ignore the present.

There's an old saying I learned somewhere. You take the reader to the unfamiliar by way of the familiar. That's why on the old quiz shows, the contestant would ask, "Is it bigger than a bread box? Smaller?" Watching or listening to television or radio, we could all picture a bread box and so we could join in the game by trying to figure out the answer to the quiz.

Memories for Everyone

"Matinee Memories," written by Ray Vodicks, appeared for the first time in the *St. Louis Post-Dispatch* and was later reprinted in *Modern Maturity,* a magazine slanted to the reading pleasure of retirees. The lead puts us back in time with:

> Picture that. The old Granada Theatre is going to reopen with a buck-a-head policy. The price may seem right in these days, but it's still a long way from the ten-cent Sunday matinees there that I remember.

103

The article goes on to describe a typical Sunday matinee at the old Granada, memories beyond the recall perhaps of many readers of the *Post-Dispatch*. But certainly the fact that the *Post-Dispatch* ran this nostalgia piece in spite of the long time-span proves my point that it isn't mandatory that a reader remember exactly what the author recalls. All young people have memories of their own Sunday matinee, and they enjoy reading about those that were before their time. The author tells us in "Matinee Memories":

> In those days, nobody worried about the sociological impact or the possible psychological damage that could be caused by watching violence on the screen, whatever that means. The big thing was that you could immerse yourself in the serial and forget about the homework and whatever chores that awaited you. It was the ultimate in escapism, which we fortunately didn't know about.

This disclosure creates reader identity—no matter what the reader's age. We all like to escape homework and tedious chores no matter how old we are.

The article concludes by circling back to the opening lead—the reference to the ten-cent Sunday matinees.

> Then came a time when we could no longer get in for a dime, and the serials seemed corny. And it was more fun to go to the early movie on Friday and Saturday night—maybe even with a girl.

The matinee was over.

ACCURACY COUNTS

Nostalgia articles don't require the exhaustive research needed in many other types of articles, such as the profile of a historical figure, or the informative how-to article. However, the nostalgia article does require accurate recall of historical events and mode of living for the time period written about.

If you're remembering the day Lindbergh flew the Atlantic, you should know who was President at the time, and the name of the plane. If you're remembering the many hours you enjoyed listening to *The Milton Berle Comedy Hour,* you should know the name of the announcer of the program, and the names of other actors and actresses in the cast. If you went to a one-room school, what kind of stove provided heat? What was the exact model of car in which you rode to that Fourth of July picnic, or to the out-of-town football game? Do you know all the names of the astronauts on the first journey to the moon?

If you're the least bit uncertain about any fact or event that occurred during the time of which you write, double-check. Your reference librarian can direct you to source material for the given years or year. History books, the Time-Life *Fabulous Century Series,* biographies, and old newspapers and periodicals are just a few of the sources available to you in checking the accuracy of your memory.

Part of the success in reaching the reader rests upon your ability to create a vivid and accurate word picture of the subject of your nostalgic memories. If something doesn't ring true, you jar the reader out of identifying with the scene you're re-creating. The nostalgic spell is broken. The reader is annoyed. "That isn't the way it was at all," he or she mutters, and immediately reaches for paper to write a letter to the editor.

Keep your memories green through deliberate methods of association, such as looking at old photographs of bygone days. Browse through old school yearbooks. Talk to old-timers whose memory of ten, twenty, thirty, or forty years ago is sharp, often sharper than their recall of what happened yesterday. Go back to a class reunion and talk about the good old days with friends who remember what you recall. You'll come home with a suitcase filled with ideas.

LET ME TELL YOU ABOUT THE TIME . . .

Like the personal experience and inspirational articles, the nostalgia article requires a warm and intimate style, a way of writing that makes the *I-You* transition. Such phrases as: Most of *us* remember with affection the first new car *we* ever bought. It's one of *your* cherished childhood memories. *My* fond memory is of a——whatever the model happened to be.

A confidential and intimate style is created with a lead that sets the nostalgic tone. Examples:

> Just remembering that long-ago day brings a warm glow.

> Sometimes, I long for the good old days when the family ate breakfast together. (Other rituals can be substituted for family breakfast hour.)

> It seems just yesterday that Grandpa gave me my first driving lesson in his old 1967 Plymouth [or whatever make of car you remember.]

The use of familiar words and phrases also helps create the confidential tone you need for a nostalgia article. Use phrases that evoke a warm, tender, even wistful emotion in your reader, phrases like—"It seems only yesterday"; "I'll never forget those lovely summer days at the beach (the mountains, on the farm)"; "The times I loved best as a kid were those stormy December days when we were home from school helping Mom bake cookies for the big day coming." Limit your nostalgic reflection to one memory, and stay with a single theme. There should be one emotional effect for the reader. If the article centers around Christmas, forget the Fourth of July. Save the fireworks for another article.

LAUGHTER IS THE BEST MEDICINE

A sense of humor is essential in writing the nostalgia article. Were the good old days really that good? Of course not. Most of us have come through traumatic experiences of one kind or another. We've suffered the pain of losing loved ones. We've been up; we've been down. There are times we'd rather forget.

The times we'd rather forget, the heart-breaking times, are not the stuff of which nostalgia is made. Memories of dark days when it took all we possessed to survive, physically or spiritually, belong in other kinds of articles such as the personal experience or the inspirational.

A sense of humor does much to help the writer and the reader capture the warm glow that is an essential ingredient of nostalgic memory, and to soften the rough edges of reality. We know there was a bad taste to the castor oil our mother gave us, but we smile as we recall her faith in this simple remedy, or as we remember how we got the stomach ache in the first place (perhaps climbing a forbidden fence to eat the neighbor's green apples).

Grandpa might have been the most difficult person in the world to live with in a day-to-day situation, but we smile now as we remember how hard we tried to win *just one* game of checkers, and never succeeded. What wouldn't we give today for one more checker game—win or lose.

Not all of your readers will have taken castor oil, nor will they have played checkers with Grandpa, but they, as well as those who *do* remember, will enjoy reading your article. Your warm emotion and your style of writing allows them to vicariously enter the scene. For a little while, they've left today's world behind and have walked into yesterday's. They're seated at that kitchen table with the checker board and all the other things you've re-created for them through your nostalgic memory.

Notebook Time

To review the qualifications for writing nostalgia:

1. A feeling for the past that enables you to evoke a response in the reader
2. The ability to select memories of the past with a *universal* interest
3. An accurate memory
4. A warm, intimate style
5. A sense of humor

If you master these qualifications, you'll succeed in stirring the reader's memory. Your lead will set the mood so that the reader leans back and sighs contentedly, prepared for a trip down memory lane. Your vivid and accurate descriptions will start your reader's own memories surfacing. A nice, simple, cozy style will make the reading easy and pleasant, and a sense of humor will bring a smile and a chuckle.

The nostalgia article is not written to change the world. It can inform or teach, but only in a gentle way. The prime purpose of a nostalgia article is to provide reader entertainment, a chance to relax at the end of a long day, a chance to daydream.

PREMISES, PREMISES

Read and clip nostalgia articles you like. Evaluate the articles. Tag the lead and notice how it takes the reader to the specific time and topic. Underline the premise or theme. Note how the article's ending usually circles back to the opening.

One of my favorite "good old days" articles appeared in the Sunday supplement of my newspaper, *The San Francisco Sunday Examiner and Chronicle*. The title clues us in to the type of piece we can expect to read: "Cars, Oh Happy Days."

The author, Edvins Beitks, sets the nostalgic mood with this lead:

> Used to be you could tell what someone was trying to say without glancing down at the back bumper to check his global politics or petty grumble or to find his sexual hoodoos hanging out. Thirty years ago you'd pull up at a drive-in stall, glance over at the dark-blue '56 Chevy with the 283 moon hubs and "Midnite Rambler" painted on the side, and know exactly what the driver was saying.

This lead sets not only the reminiscent mood, but gives us a vivid and accurate word picture of the particular vintage car that the author remembers. He goes on to describe other cars, such as the "gray and pink Pontiac next to you that meant 'this is the folks' car and I've got to be in by eleven.' "

We catch a glimpse of a "chromed out '35 Model A," which according to the author told the world the owner had left high school for the assembly line but couldn't give up the Friday night cruise.

As I said before, nostalgia articles must make a link or connection between the present and the past. In this article about cars of another day, the author provides us with a transition when he says,

> New cars still say things, true. A BMW is talking a different language from a Porsche, a Volvo station wagon is a starter-turn from a VW Rabbit.

Next comes the comparison which, in memory at least, makes the "good old days" seem more worthy of affection.

Referring to new cars, the author continues:

> But it's a factory picture turned out hundreds at a time. In the old days, when Detroit walked the world in seven-league boots, it didn't take two hours sitting in a driveway before a new Chevy was yanked out of assembly-line land and told to sit up and speak in street jargon.

A comparison is made of other car-related experiences, such as an order of a "buck-29's worth of burgers and fries." The author tells us that the drive-ins have gone the way of the orange-juice stand and movie theaters made up to look like a "hookah dream." There are only a handful left now. After taking us on the journey to how it was in the days when the author checked out the '56 Chevy, the article concludes by telling us that the few drive-ins left are drawing on the middle-aged driver now, the middle-aged and the high-schoolers who "still let their cars do the talking for them." (Again connection between present and past.)

But it's not like the nights when a Pontiac 389 turned heads as soon as the sound of it rumbled across the stalls. These days they [the drive-ins] are frequented by people locked into imports and cube-like cars. It's like they're making a pilgrimage to the Sacred Burial Ground, sifting through the off-white bones of Detroit's supercharged elephants, listening for the ghost cough of a four-barrel rattling around the parking lot before it's drowned out by the tinny sound of passing traffic; people driving by on their way to pick up chicken-under-heating-lamp at some triple-level shopping center salad bar, taking it home in time to see a rerun of "Happy Days."

I think you'll agree this article meets the requirements for a good nostalgia piece. The style fits the subject, old cars. The memory recall is accurate. There's plenty of humor. And for a little while, at least, we believe the cars and cruising in the good old days were more fun.

SELLING YESTERDAY

Many magazines and newspapers use nostalgia articles. My three examples came from a variety of sources: a daily column, a Sunday supplement section, and a magazine popular with retired people as well as those looking forward to retirement, *Modern Maturity.*

Other markets would include religious publications of various faiths, family-type periodicals such as *Grit,* and even men's magazines where the nostalgia might relate to action and adventure, as in a memory of a first hunting trip with Dad, or the day a father took his son out fishing for the first time.

If you'll take a little time to study market requirements in your *Writer's Market,* and watch for market guidelines in your monthly issues of *The Writer* and *Writer's Digest,* you'll find listings of numerous publications looking for well-written nostalgia articles. *The Saturday Evening Post* often runs this type of piece.

At various holiday times, many magazines set the nostalgic tone with covers depicting an old-fashioned, traditional celebration of the holiday, and the contents invariably include a nostalgia article.

Keep the various seasons in mind and work at least six months ahead; that is, have your Christmases Past article ready to mail in *May*. A good time to begin to write seasonal pieces is as close to a particular holiday as possible so as to capture the right mood. And then mail at least six months ahead of time.

Since the nostalgia article is so personal, there's no need to query beforehand. What you remember and how you feel about what you remember is exclusive to you. Therefore, an editor needs to see the manuscript to make a decision.

When you see listed a market wanting nostalgia articles, or any other type you're interested in writing, don't forget to send for the sample issue—often free. There's no substitute for reading the publication itself to get the slant (focus), style, and editorial preference as to article format.

I can't guarantee that you'll get rich writing nostalgia articles. When you're first starting, more than likely you'll be selling to the smaller publications. Even at this point, however, unexpected bonuses can come to you through reprint publication. *Reader's Digest* frequently reprints a *good* nostalgia article, one with a strong reader identification.

The greatest reward you receive in writing about the good old days is in the many opportunities you have to relive in memory some of the happiest days of your life. In so doing, on paper, you can help thousands of other people savor the same pleasure.

RECORDING YESTERDAY

Now that you've read this chapter, sit back, close your eyes and let your thoughts wander back along the road to yesterday. When you come to a particularly memorable place, one that makes you feel warm and sentimental, put a piece of paper in your typewriter and start writing.

In the first draft, let it all hang out. Write from your heart. Later, you can check your draft against the suggestions given here, and make necessary revisions.

Nostalgia articles are easy to write, a chance to relax from perhaps a far more difficult project. They're also one of the nicest ways for writers to develop their sensory skills and use their talents to bring reading pleasure to others. Try sharing the fragrance from the roses in *your* garden of memory.

CHECKLIST FOR YOUR NOSTALGIA ARTICLES

☑Did you choose a universal subject, one with meaning for a great number of people?

☑Have you painted vivid word pictures by drawing upon the five senses? Did you include the smells, sights, textures, sounds, and tastes of the good old days?

☑Have you softened the rough edges of yesterday with a touch of humor?

☑Did you compare and contrast the past with the present to make the connection for younger readers?

☑Have you checked all facts and details you're unsure of or can't remember?

See the World—
Writing
the Travel Article

The travel article is one of the most enjoyable ways in which you can write what you know and get paid for it. All it takes is a little gypsy blood in your veins, a sturdy notebook, a camera, and a destination.

When I made my first trip to England, I got an assignment from my local paper to do a weekly travel series. Daily notes in my looseleaf notebook became a weekly feature in my local paper, and led to many other writing assignments. Later, the six articles gave me the background information I needed to write my first romance novel, *Nurse Abroad.*

This series of travel articles taught me a valuable lesson, something I've carried into all my writing and into my teaching: If you're excited and enthusiastic about what you see and do, if you can write it down in easy-to-understand words that convey your excitement and enthusiasm to others, you'll turn other people on. And you'll sell what you write.

There are almost as many ways to write a travel article as there are places to visit. In this chapter I'll discuss four mainstays of this type: off-the-beaten path articles, new slants on well-known places, event-oriented places, and travel profiles.

In any travel article the purpose is to sell travel. You sell travel by bringing the reader's attention to something of special interest about a particular place. This interest can be generated by the place itself, its beauty and picturesque location; by colorful and exciting events scheduled within its boundaries; or by the famous and infamous people who have lived in this place and left their mark upon it.

SECRET HIDEAWAYS

First, there is the type known as the *off-the-beaten-path* travel article. This is a wonderful kind of article to write if you haven't written travel pieces before.

Off-the-beaten-path articles are easier to write because you're not in competition with hundreds of other writers doing articles on well-known places such as Disneyland, Hawaii, Marine World USA, or the Pyramids.

115

This little-known place you're writing about might be known only to you and your family, and perhaps to a few long-time residents of the area: a little family-type campground not inundated by tourists; a country road paralleling the freeway but seldom traveled because it's been forgotten since the superhighway straightened out all the curves; a quiet, isolated beach ideal for sunbathing in private.

"Arkansas Odyssey," by Paul Hemphill (*Reader's Digest,* September '84) is a good example of an off-the-beaten path article. In it, Hemphill describes how he and his son traveled the length of the Arkansas River, camping along the river bank and walking through small towns.

Hemphill writes movingly about the changes the river journey made in him and his son. In conclusion, he says his son wants to spend another summer working the Arkansas River.

> And maybe, in another generation, he'll bring a son back to the place of his youth, so another Hemphill can learn from the river.
>
> The river will still be there.

This very different travel piece is sure to inspire other fathers to journey with their sons on their own odyssey.

A great many people like the adventure of discovering new places, places not overcrowded and overpriced. All you have to do is point them in the right direction. Tell how you came upon this hideaway bed-and-breakfast place located off the busy highway on the edge of some town. The owners don't want to cater to the whole world; they're content to give relaxation and pleasure to a few appreciative travelers.

One of my students, Mary Priest, found a market for her off-the-beaten-path article on the pleasure of visiting small wineries within thirty-five miles of San Francisco, along the sixty-five-mile stretch of Redwood Highway. She took her own photographs for her piece, titled, "Days of Wine and Redwoods," which appeared in the Sunday supplement section of the *San Francisco Chronicle.*

Any time you can write enthusiastically about some intriguing place or event, perhaps to be seen and enjoyed after an easy Sunday drive from a major city or its surrounding areas, you have a salable article for a local newspaper or a regional magazine, maybe even an in-flight publication.

As an example, on my last flight on AIRCAL, I picked up their in-flight magazine and read a short piece about the Chinese Culture Center in San Francisco and the special exhibits to be seen there. I've lived in the San Francisco Bay Area for over twenty-five years, but I've never seen the Chinese Culture Center. Since reading the article, I've put it on my must-see list.

Often exciting material for travel articles is just over the fence. Look around. You'll see what I mean—a Chinese Culture Center you never knew about before you started looking.

MAIN ATTRACTIONS

The second type of travel article features a well-known tourist attraction such as the Grand Canyon, the Great Wall of China, or the French Riviera. The information you give your readers in this type of article must be something they haven't read a hundred times before.

As an example of a fresh slant on a well-known place, "Easygoing Puerto Rico" is the title of a travel feature in a recent issue of *The Saturday Evening Post,* written by Jo and Rod Williams. The fresh approach in this piece is in the description of Puerto Rico as a perfect place to get away and enjoy a relaxing vacation, free from stress. Many people think of Puerto Rico as romantic and exciting, but not necessarily relaxing. So the authors have brought us a fresh slant on a vacation possibility.

A writer friend of mine, Judy Davis, found the something different for her travel article when she decided to bicycle through Baja, California. There have been many other articles on Baja, articles written about the food, shopping, the danger in drinking the water, and how to get there by plane or car. How many people have seen Baja from a bicycle?

The article appeared in *True* magazine under the title, "Bicycling Through Baja."

Finding a New Angle

I've already mentioned Mary Priest, who toured the small wineries in her backyard and then wrote and sold an article on the subject. When she made a trip to England with her husband, she studied the markets before she left, and then during her journey, kept her eyes and ears open for the something different that would result in salable travel articles.

When she returned from England, Mary wrote and sold not one but several articles to different markets, all out of her one travel experience abroad.

The following is a list of her sales, each article about some facet of English life as *she* saw it. (Notice how she was able to sell the same article twice, to noncompetitive markets.)

"Pennywise Dining"	*International Travel News*
"Salisbury and Her Cathedral"	*Trip and Tour, International Travel News*
"'Longleat House"	*Trip and Tour, Western World*
"Shopping With the Natives"	*International Travel News*
"Those English Gardens"	*The Record*
"Longleat House"	*International Travel News*
"Museum of London"	*International Travel News*
"English Manor Houses"	*Airfair*
"Avebury"	*International Travel News*
"Don't Stand in the Zebra"	*International Travel News*
(Pedestrian Lane)	

The subjects in Mary's articles derived from her trip to England have been covered by other writers—*but* she found new things to say about them. Mary explains how she finds the fresh slant this way:

I look for the unexpected. From my research *before* I leave home, I have a preconceived idea of what a place will be like. I know its attractions and shortcomings. When I arrive at my destination, or even *en route,* I keep constantly on the alert for the pluses or minuses I did not anticipate.

For example, the idea for my article, "Those English Gardens," came to me while I was looking out from our hotel room window in the town of Salisbury into the vegetable garden back of a neighboring house, and I thought of how pleasantly surprised we had been at the variety of fresh vegetables we had been served at every small hotel and country inn where we had stopped. I recalled all the window boxes I'd seen filled with herbs and vegetable gardens, and how sometimes even front yards would be given over to the growing of vegetables.

I knew that the subject of English gardens with their beautiful flowers had been well covered by other writers. So I decided to write an article, not about England's flower gardens, but about the *vegetable* gardens of England.

The full title of Mary's garden article when it appeared in *The Record,* a newspaper published in New Jersey, was "Those English Gardens are a Vegetarian's Delight."

There are several ways in which you can get a new approach to a popular, well-known place. Your beforehand research about this place will have given you a good base. You'll know what's already been said. With this information in mind, you can start looking for the *new* the moment you arrive at your destination.

Talk to the natives. Strike up conversations everywhere you go—in coffee shops, on tour buses, at the local library and Chamber of Commerce, and at service stations when you stop to refuel your car. Service station operators can often direct you to some special event or point of interest you might have missed.

FOR A LIMITED TIME ONLY

A third type of travel article highlights an event that takes place in a certain town or city on a specific date. These pieces are popular with local and regional publications. If the subject is exciting enough and has universal interest, it can find a market in a general-readership magazine such as *The Saturday Evening Post,* or in a special-interest magazine such as *Modern Maturity* or *True.*

As an example of universal interest, most people enjoy getting out to various kinds of festivals, fairs, parades, and commemorative events. Can you tell them about the blessing of the fleet in a coastal town, or the celebration of the gathering of the crops in an agricultural area?

Various holidays, especially Christmas, lend themselves to travel articles, with each section of the country having special events. The Dickens Fair in San Francisco draws a tremendous crowd during the holiday season, and every year articles about this occasion appear in the local paper, in Sunday supplements, and in regionally slanted magazines such as *Sunset* and *San Francisco* magazine.

In May, Sacramento sponsors one of the largest jazz festivals in the world, and again articles start appearing a month before the festival. Some tell people how to get to Old Sacramento, the historic site of the festival, some describe the various jazz groups who will play, or give information on other interesting things to see in the capital city.

Wherever you live, throughout the year there are exciting events you can write about. Pay attention to coming attractions and learn everything you can about what interests you. Remember that an article covering a scheduled occasion held on a certain date must be submitted at least two to six months in advance of the occasion. If you're too late this year to meet an editor's deadline for submission, attend the event anyway, write the article, and submit it when the right time rolls around next year. You'll have to do a few minor revisions to bring your article up to date, but that won't take much time.

NATIVE SONS AND DAUGHTERS

The travel profile is the fourth type of travel article you can write and sell to travel publications and general-interest types of magazines. Travel profiles follow much the same format as the profile articles I discussed in Chapter Three. The difference is in the slant of the subject matter. The person you write about must have, or have had, a strong influence on a particular area, to meet the requirements of a travel article; to highlight this influence, you can usually find a museum, library, or other site set aside as the town's tribute to its distinguished native son or daughter. The special place of tribute will provide you with a wealth of material.

Your subject must have more than local or regional fame if you want to reach the national circulation publications. The profile must be of someone widely known, a celebrity or a national hero or heroine. When subjects are not well known, what they do must be extremely exciting and hold universal interest.

Make a list of possible travel articles you could do about celebrated people, associated with their sections of the country. Here are a few possibilities to get you started:

Ansel Adams—Yosemite National Park
Presidential libraries—Truman, Eisenhower, Kennedy, Eleanor Roosevelt.
Charles Lindbergh—The resting place of *The Spirit of St. Louis.* The Smithsonian Institution.
Howard Hughes—Site of the "Spruce Goose," Long Beach, California.
Charles Russell-Western Art Gallery in Great Falls, Montana.

Think about writers and their birthplaces: Jack London Museum and Park, Glen Ellen, California; Margaret Mitchell, Atlanta, Georgia; Thomas Wolfe's home, Asheville, North Carolina; Nathaniel Hawthorne's house, Seven Gables, Salem, Massachusetts.

Consider inventors, such as Thomas Edison and Alexander Graham Bell, and the museums dedicated to them in their hometowns.

The list goes on and on. These famous people have been written about time and again, but they'll continue to make copy for travel magazines because readers want to see where they lived and where they worked.

Not all colorful and interesting "characters" of a given place have museums named after them, but they still make good travel profile material, enhancing the atmosphere and mood of the area through the tales told about them by the natives who love to spin a yarn about the "old-timer."

Interesting people, known and unknown, add to local color and are as much a part of the landscape as are the mountains, rivers, and lakes. Remember to look them up when you visit a place and then weave these old-timers into your travel pieces. There's an old saying in journalism: "People make news." The saying applies equally to travel writing.

KNOW YOUR READER

The same key that opens the door to publication in other types of articles will help you sell your travel articles. That key to success is a thorough knowledge of the market.

To know the market means to understand the needs of its readership. As in other types of articles, the reader's general age group, educational background, economic status, activities and hobbies, and physical limitations will determine your choice of subject, your approach, and your style.

Keep the reader constantly before you as you write. Reader awareness not only increases your chances of selling the article you've just completed, but it opens up other opportunities for taking the same subject and writing it again from a different angle for other types of readers.

For instance, the travel article you'd write for the college student on touring Europe is not the article you'd write for *Modern Maturity.* The college student is usually in vigorous health and is interested in physical adventure, while the senior citizen often has some physical limitation which needs to be considered in planning any trek away from the comfort and security of home.

Young people often consider roughing it all a part of the adventure of travel. Many young people travel through Europe with packs on their backs, sleeping in youth hostels or camping out. They like to travel in twos and threes or in groups; often their mode of transportation is on bicycle or motorcycle, or even on foot. Older people have the same curiosity and love of adventure as do younger travelers, but like to explore at a more leisurely pace and usually with a measure of comfort.

Most senior-age travelers are semiretired or retired, and so have more time to spend on the road. While bicycling or motorcycling through Baja, California, or through Europe might not appeal to most of this group, the adventure found in traveling in vans, recreational vehicles, and motor homes is an exciting prospect.

For both young and not-so-young travelers, cost is often an item, and so travel information should emphasize the economy factor.

There are other groups of tourists with special needs and interests, such as the parents of young children who must plan their vacations around the problems of keeping their offspring entertained on a long trip. They are interested in places to stay and things to see that would be interesting to children as well as to adults.

People travel with pets, and pets require special consideration, whether the journey be of one day's duration or a typical two-week vacation. Among the article titles featured on the cover of the September '84 issue of *The Saturday Evening Post* is one slanted toward the traveler with pets—"Travel Tips for Fido." If you've ever traveled with your Fido, you could have written that article.

Another group of people interested in seeing the world has extra special needs—wheelchair travelers. Any article you could write telling this readership how to overcome the obstacles in places where their needs are overlooked, will find a market in a variety of general interest magazines, as well as in health-oriented publications such as *Health* and *Prevention.*

STUDY THE MARKETS

The best way to learn the needs of various travel magazines is to spend some time browsing at the magazine stands or in the library. You'll see that all travel magazines cover the subject of where to go and what to see, but each has a different focus, a slant dictated by the needs and interests of its readership.

Travel pieces for newspaper Sunday supplements are family-oriented, while those in singles publications take into consideration the needs of the solo traveler who is often venturing alone for the first time.

In-flight magazines for air travelers usually cater to the special needs of the businessman or businesswoman who may have time to kill between flights. In-flight publications feature articles on recommended hotels, the best places to dine, and what can be seen along the routes covered by the particular airline.

Beneath the cover title of the magazine you'll often find a short blurb or phrase that clues the reader to the type of travel articles presented in its pages.

Travel-Holiday announces on its cover that it is "The Magazine That Roams the Globe." The lead article featured on the cover usually reinforces the global theme, such as an article titled, "Shanghai—A World Apart."

In contrast to the global magazine, *Alaska,* a regional periodical, proclaims itself to be "The Magazine on Life on the Last Frontier," and the cover illustration depicts a wintry scene with a dog team mushing its way over an icy terrain.

Taking the time to study the covers of magazines can give you one of your first lessons in learning the meaning of the word *slant.* The reader is first drawn to the cover. If interested, he or she will open the magazine.

Your next step in getting to know the slant of a travel publication is to pay attention to the table of contents page. There article titles are repeated, augmented by captions designed to hook the reader's interest. As an example, one article in an issue of *Alaska,* titled "The Dream and the Reality," by Jeff Schultz, has a caption reading, "Danger, determination, endurance, exhausting achievement—all these spell Iditarod."

The photographs accompanying a travel article are important in awakening the reader's interest in the subject matter. Pictures draw you into the scene and make you wish you were there, gazing out at the harbor, riding horseback along a mountain trail, or basking on some sun-drenched beach far away from the daily grind. The number and quality of photographs demonstrate the probable requirements of the market you hope to write for.

Check Them Out

If you are not experienced in the art of travel writing, get the feel of it first by studying what others have written and published. You'll be far more confident when you begin your first travel piece. The following is an evaluation list for published travel articles. (You can use it to judge the effectiveness of your own travel writing as well.

1. What type of lead was used? Descriptive? Informative? Anecdotal? Dialogue?

Many travel articles begin with a tantalizing description of some exotic place, the kind of description that makes you want to put the cover on your typewriter and pack your bags.

"Hawaii," by Georgia Hesse, appeared in *National Geographic* magazine, and is a good example of a mouth-watering lead.

> Evening in Hawaii. The sky has turned deep purple, the shade of the inside of an orchid. The air is moist, fragrant, and pulsing with possibilities. The moment catches me on the lanai (veranda) at Kona Village Resort, which is situated on a lava flow several miles from the town of Kailua-Kona.
>
> That sky falls imperceptibly into the sea. There is no earth-ocean division, except where black rocks poke up and white spray (caught in a spotlight halo) dazzles into the glare, smashes against the stone teeth and slides, hissing, back into black.

Who wouldn't want to go to Hawaii after reading that lovely description?

If you like to write lush, poetic description, you'll delight in writing the kind of travel articles where vivid word pictures of the beauty of a place are an important lure in selling travel.

In contrast to this descriptive lead, Judy Davis's article, "Bicycling Through Baja," begins with an informative lead appropriate to the subject.

> Until recently, tourist travel in Baja, California, was limited to four-wheel-drive vehicles traveling in pairs and equipped with spare parts. The only road—El Camino—snaking through the mountainous 1000-mile-long desert penisula wasn't even entirely graded, let alone paved. But Mexico has begun paving El Camino and now southern Baja—Baja del Sur—is open to adventurers with ten-speed bicycles and the urge to seek a challenging vacation.

The article in *Alaska* about "Chickaloon Mountain Man," a travel profile, begins with a lead that immediately characterizes the subject of the article.

> The Chickaloon Mountain Man says he once took a job. He made that claim on a rainy September afternoon to a group of hunters gathered at his camp in the Talkeetna Mountains. One or two looked doubtful, but their guide was known for telling truths stranger than any fiction that comes out of the wilderness.
>
> The mountain man stuck a hand in a pocket of his baggy, patched jeans, raised his mug, chewed on a sip of thick coffee, spat out some grounds, grimaced, and told the story.

After reading about John Luster, the adventure-loving travel readers will most likely want to take off for Alaska—if only in dreams.

To get on with our evaluation list:

2. What words conveyed the beauty, color, excitement, of the place, the event, or (if applicable) the profile subject?

Be a story teller when you write your travel articles. Create word pictures through sensory imagery.

Use your five senses in your description. It's not enough to tell readers that a village was "quaint" unless you let them see, hear, smell, feel, and taste the quaintness.

Vivid description is the life's blood of good travel writing. Select your words carefully. They are the only mode of transportation you have to take your reader *there*. Let the reader know how the newly cut hay smells on a June morning, and how the wind sounded as it whispered through the tall pine trees. Let the reader's mouth drool as you describe that bacon sizzling in the pan over a campfire, let him hear the murmur of the ocean waves, and see them breaking in a long ribbon of white against the golden sand.

Make a list of key words that create word pictures. Look for words such as golden, sizzling, smoking, moist, fragrant, pulsing.

3. What was the theme of the travel article?

Sometimes the theme will reflect a different mode of travel, as in Judy Davis's bicycling through Baja. It can be in the charm of a little-known, off-the-byway retreat you've discovered. The theme might be your personal approach to a place.

Georgia Hesse tells us her theme. She prepares us by telling us first:

> I shiver despite the warmth and imagine beasts alive in the grasses, ghosts in the sand. (I know there are spirits alive in the sea.) The world beyond this small island dot ceases to matter; maybe even to exist. . . .

Then comes the theme line:

> Make believe is the message of Hawaii.

Always look for the theme sentence when you study travel articles. Then when you get an idea for a place you want to write about, practice writing themes. If you had to describe this place in one sentence, how would you do it? What left the greatest impression on you?

4. What was covered in the body of the article?

In well-written travel articles you'll find plenty of solid, helpful information. You'll often find specific suggestions on the best way to get to a certain place, the best time to go, the cost of going by several modes of transportation, along with the cost of staying overnight or for a typical week or two-week vacation. Usually budget accommodation costs are given, along with prices of more luxurious lodgings.

When you study published travel articles, make a list of the various kinds of information you find. Later, when you check through your notes, compare the amount of information in your article with the amount in the published pieces.

After you've written your rough draft, check for solid substance. Does it seem thin compared with your role models? If so, do some additional research. If possible, go back to the setting of your article to gather more material. If you can't go back (it isn't always possible to jump on a plane and fly away to the other side of the world), write to relatives or friends who live there. Other sources of current information are the many visitor outlets, as for example, Chamber of Commerce, civic organizations, and travel bureaus. Historical and genealogical societies are happy to help you with your research.

I can't overstress the importance of making sure your information on a particular place is *current.*

To show you what can happen if you don't bring your research up to date, I'll tell you about my own experience. I keep a file folder on each geographical place I think I might use in either my nonfiction or fiction writing. Since I grew up in Southern California that folder bulges with material on Los Angeles, San Diego, and La Jolla, my girlhood home. As part of the San Diego research I include clippings on Tijuana, the Mexican border town. Some of the clippings are yellowing with age.

I hadn't seen Tijuana in many years until I went to San Diego recently to give a speech for the San Diego Chapter of the Romance Writers of America.

"How would you like to have dinner in Tijuana?" my hostess asked me.

"I'd love it!" I answered.

"You won't know it," she said. "It's all changed."

Tijuana had changed indeed. The shabby, dusty little border town with its street vendors and sidewalk stalls was gone, along with narrow streets and modest store fronts. Tijuana was now a beautiful contemporary city with wide tree-lined boulevards. Modern high-rise buildings filled the skyline.

"It looks more like Los Angeles or San Francisco," was my comment, when we had parked the car and were entering the biggest (three blocks long) supermarket I'd ever seen.

When I returned home, I threw out all the dated clippings on Tijuana and replaced them with up-to-the-minute Chamber of Commerce brochures and street maps. I shuddered to think of the egg that would have been on my face if I'd written about this now lovely city purely from my nostalgic memories.

Moral: Don't trust your memory. The world is changing too fast. Even six months can make a *big* difference. Condominiums and high-rise apartments have a way of crowding out the open fields of our nostalgic recollections.

5. How did the article end?

Authors usually briefly summarize important points in the article's conclusion, then add one or two more exciting new facts that will make the reader want to see, explore, or vacation at this fascinating place.

The theme is usually restated also. In "Hawaii," Georgia Hesse concludes with this restatement of her theme:

> The land falls away at your feet into an eternity of green, edged by the shimmering sea. It is enough to make you believe in Menehunes, Pele, Maui, Kane, Kaneloa, Lono . . .

The Hawaiian words refer to legends about the various sites throughout the island, and tie in with her theme of "make believe." The last view the author gives the reader is of the Islands as seen from a helicopter—a different final glance.

THE TRAVEL WRITER'S EQUIPMENT

Your camera will give you an accurate picture of the places you've seen and the people you've met and interviewed. If your camera is a couple of years old, have it checked at a camera store. Take along a good supply of batteries for the flash if your camera uses them, and of course, plenty of film. Supplies bought at home are much less expensive than what you pick up in little out-of-the-way places, or abroad. There's no greater panic known to a travel writer than to come across an exciting picture subject, aim the camera, click, and then find out you've run out of film, and have no replacement.

Your tape recorder can serve you in several ways. You need it for interviews certainly, but it is also invaluable to you as you fly or ride across the country, and even the ocean. When you see something interesting, or an exciting thought hits you, talk into your recorder. Capture your enthusiasm through your voice as well as through the notes you frantically scribble down. If you can't take notes (and there are many situations in which you can't), talk into your recorder, and then play your tape back when you get to your motel or hotel and make notes from the tape you made on the wing. Make sure your recorder is in top working condition and take plenty of tapes or cassettes. You can't have too many.

In addition to camera and tape recorder, as a travel writer you'll need a travel-oriented reference library, geographies, maps, a globe, and good travel guidebooks such as Fodor's travel guides on various countries of the world.

Your travel reference library doesn't have to cost you a fortune. Library sales, secondhand stores, thrift outlets, all are rich sources of travel books, atlases, and even a globe. If you find a Fodor Guidebook that is a year or two old, grab it. The basic information on climate, vegetation, places to go, stay, and eat remain the same for quite a long time. You can update any outdated information with current editions you browse through at your library, or from articles appearing in current magazines.

THE TRAVELER WRITER

The question arises, do you have to go to places in order to write about them?

In my opinion you do. Travel articles are more than ency-clopedic accounts, giving bare facts and statistics on a geo-graphical location. A good travel article transfers an emotional impact from the writer to the reader—an intimate sharing of the joy and excitement found in visiting a certain place, whether near or far away, well known or off the beaten path.

You might research until you know a place as you know your own backyard, but it would be impossible to capture a truly fresh insight unless you had actually been there.

Writers look at the subjects of their travel articles, no mat-ter what types they write, through their own personal viewfin-ders, eyes unlike any others. Writers respond to the places they see with fresh insight, and it is this very *personal* feeling about travel subjects that sets one article apart from another. No two writers see the same thing in the same way. It's the *dif-ference* in what we see in places and in people that the editor of any publication looks for constantly.

No place has been written about more than the Hawaiian Islands, and articles about this Pacific paradise will continue to fill the pages of all kinds of magazines. But each article will be just a little different from all the others before and those to come after, because of a particular writer's viewfinder.

BON VOYAGE!

The next time you plan your vacation, whether it be to your fa-vorite fishing stream a few miles from home or to some far-away city on the Nile, take time to jot down some notes on possible travel pieces you could write when you return. Pre-planning your travel article subjects is as important as is good preparation for the journey itself.

Take this book with you on your trip and refresh your memory by reading this chapter again. Jot down your impres-sions of everything you see, including the kinds of people who live in this place that you're visiting or sight-seeing.

Be thinking of a good sharp lead—a sentence or two, or a short paragraph that would capture the colorful and exciting aura of the place for the reader.

Think theme. A theme usually evolves from a feeling about a place, something beyond the visual beauty or historical background. Theme has to do with the character of a place, its *essence.*

If you've never written travel articles before, start by submitting to your local paper. Local editors are always looking for good travel articles to brighten up the pages of their daily, weekly, and Sunday supplement publications. Before you begin your trip, take the time to talk with the editor of your local paper. Tell him or her where you're going and that you'd like to write an article for the paper.

If you know your travel plans far enough in advance, you can query travel and general-interest magazines as well, and very often get a "green light," an indication of editorial interest in an article on your travel adventure. At the time you write the editor of the magazine, be sure you ask for a guidesheet showing editorial requirements and the specific interests of the readership.

You don't have to travel to Europe or other faraway places to get into travel writing. There are plenty of subjects near your own home, which is far away to people who are far away!

Too, you can use your vacation experiences, your Sunday drives, and your knowledge of interesting nearby places to write local travel articles that may have a universal appeal. Just remember to infuse your writing with your own genuine enthusiasm, excitement, and pride, and write in such a way that these emotions transfuse the reader with the same feelings.

Try it! You might be surprised how much you like it, and how far it takes you as a professional writer.

CHECKLIST FOR TRAVEL ARTICLES

☑️If your article is about a well-known place, do you give a new slant? Did your research turn up some new and interesting information that will make the reader want to go there again, or encourage a trip there if he hasn't yet visited the location?

☑️If the destination is off the beaten path, have you given the reader enough reasons for going?

☑️Does your article give practical information on such facts as the time required to get there, the best road to travel—if by car; alternate modes of travel (the reader may not want to drive or can't)? Do you include a choice of accommodations with approximate cost per night, as well as the price of food at the lodging and along the way?

☑️Have you documented your information either through personal experience or through careful research?

☑️Is your article timely? Did you submit far enough in advance to hit the *vacation* magazine or newspaper market? (Six months in advance of a summer issue is not too soon to submit. Travel publications use more material for peak seasonal issues.)

☑️Do you have good black-and-white pictures to illustrate your article, or transparencies of color photos?

☑️Did you stay within the word length for the markets to which you're submitting?

☑️What is your plus value? How is your article different from others written about the same place?

☑️Does your piece provide unusual facts and vivid description, making the reader want to pack his bags and go to your Shangri-la, Island Paradise, or exciting city?

☑️Is your style right for the travel market? Have you used the five senses in your description so that the reader can see, hear, smell, touch, and taste the many delights to be found along the journey and at the end of the trail?

In-Depth and in Jest— Writing Think and Humor Articles

The last two easiest-to-write article types require special kinds of talent and experience. That's why I saved them for last. The think article is usually a serious attempt on the part of the writer to bring the reader's attention to problems of political, social, philosophical, or religious concern. The humor piece, on the other hand, can take the very same problems and, through humorous treatment rather than serious, capture a reader's attention and make a point.

THINK IT OVER

You may not consider yourself a *serious* writer, either by talent or experience, and therefore, you may be tempted to skip over this discussion. If this is your feeling, I urge you to stay with me, and I'll tell you why. You never know when in your career you'll need to write your opinions about a situation or problem in a serious, in-depth way.

You may be called upon to write a think piece as a part of your professional or job duties. An organization you belong to, knowing you're a writer, may need you to present its position on a local issue. Charitable organizations such as March of Dimes, the American Cancer Society, and the Red Cross need people with writing talent and experience to write brochures and campaign literature. Your contribution as someone who can put thoughts into words is a valuable asset to any organization or profession.

If you're running for office at the local, state, or national level, you can put yourself out in front of other candidates through your ability to voice your position on issues, and also through your writing talents.

Finally, the more you know about all kinds of writing, the better chances you'll have for surviving in a highly competitive profession. What you learn about one field of writing you can always use in another.

SOUNDING OFF ON THE PET PEEVE

There are several ways in which you can write opinion pieces on a variety of problems that plague us all. One of the easiest ways is by writing the *pet peeve,* also known as the *sound-off.*

When my students complain about some situation that makes them angry, I tell them, "Don't let this give you an ulcer. Write a pet peeve about it and bring it to class next week." Many of them have published their pet peeves.

We all experience frustrating situations and irritating behavior on the part of relatives, friends, and associates that make us want to climb the walls. Our reaction to these annoyances can vary from a few grumbles to an all-out explosion. We let off steam to anyone who will listen, and then we go about our business until the next peeve comes along. Oral expression seldom does much to change the situation, but written words can effect changes.

If something upsets you, write your feelings into a pet peeve. Sound off about the situation. Send what you write to the Letters to the Editor department of your local paper, or to one of the suitable feature departments of your favorite magazine. Speaking out can help reduce stress, and you might possibly get a little check. Perhaps your sound-off article will draw enough attention to inspire a solution to the problem.

As an example of how effective a pet peeve type of opinion or think piece can be, an elderly student in one of my classes was upset because she'd almost been knocked down by a bike rider while strolling along the sidewalk on the main street in her town.

"Write a sound-off," I told her.

She did, mailed it off to the Letters to the Editor section of the local paper, and in a few days her piece was published. Other letters poured in expressing the same feelings. As a result, the City Fathers posted more warning signs against bike riders on sidewalks and enforced the penalty for those who ignored the signs.

You may not be bothered by this problem, but I'm sure

you have other situations that annoy you. Start a list of these peeves in your notebook.

Peeves are not great issues. Nations don't rise and fall because of them. They are the small grains of sand that wear away our patience.

To get you started with your list, here are a few peeves I've listed in my notebook.

People Peeves

1. Neighbors who vibrate your walls with the high volume of their stereo or television.
2. Neighbors in an apartment or condominium complex who park their car in your space, then disappear from the face of the earth for hours or days.
3. People who tell the same story over and over again—usually a dull tale.
4. People who are always late.
5. People who arrive an hour early, catching you with after-five-o'clock shadow or hair rollers, as the case may be.
6. Hostesses who know you're on a diet and heap your plate as though famine were about to descend on the land.
7. People who borrow and never return.
8. People you visit who keep their television on, making intelligent social conversation impossible.
9. Relatives and friends who know you are a writer and still open a telephone conversation with, "I hope I'm not interrupting your work," and then proceed to talk for an hour.
10. People who write you letters after a six-month silence and ask you, "Did you hear about what happened to Mary and Ted? I haven't time to tell you now, but I'll write all about it in my next letter." Another six months wait. When you receive the next letter, there's not a single word about Mary and Ted.

I'm sure you've experienced one or two of these people-oriented experiences, any one of which can cause you to gnash your teeth and pull your hair.

Situation Peeves

1. The office or company party, usually Christmas or New Year's. Watch it! The boss is hovering. There ought to be a law prohibiting such occasions.
2. Banks that want to replace warm-bodied employees with cold-blooded, faceless machines.
3. Other people's mail continually deposited in your mailbox by the same mail carrier.
4. Christmas cards with only a signature and no news.
5. Christmas brag letters. Husband's been promoted to vice president. Wife named mother of the year. Kids top of honor roll and winners of coveted scholarships. (Your husband has just been let go. Your son had his driving privileges taken away—again. Your daughter just informed you she's pregnant—no marriage plans.)
6. Old "rustic" houses sold at six times their original value. Also fixer-uppers with ceilings falling down, and termites breakdancing in the walls.
7. Telephones that ring in the dead of night with blurry voices on the line asking to speak to Mabel or Harry, who don't live at your house and never did.
8. Waitresses and waiters who make you feel invisible.
9. Word processors that inform you, "No more room on the disk" just when the creative juices are flowing copiously.
10. Typewriters that break down, needing a week in the shop when you're facing a deadline.

I'm sure you can relate to one or more of these situations which, while not of earth-shaking proportions, can cause you to either silently or aloud give vent to your favorite cussword.

Again, as in all the article types we've discussed in this book, the peeve must have universal identification, must be a situation that bothers a lot of people.

GET IT OUT OF YOUR SYSTEM

No matter how angry you are at some clod who has ruined your day, or at some situation, you must calm down before you start to write. While turbulent and justified emotion can trigger the idea for your pet peeve or sound-off piece, like any other article, what you write requires something besides hot air.

A touch of humor often tones down the darker emotion of anger that might turn many people off. A light touch is needed when writing this type of article. If you come down too heavily on the culprit or situation that caused your anger, you'll come off as a crank or troublemaker.

Start as you would for any other article—with a good strong lead. In the lead, you set the scene, the how and where it all happened, and state the cause of your annoyance.

The elderly student, justifiably upset by the bike rider who almost knocked her down, started her piece by describing how she loved being able to walk to town from her house, enjoying the balmy summer days as she browsed in store windows. In the thirty or more years she'd lived in the town, she'd always felt safe walking along the main street. Until a few days ago when. . . . She then described in dramatic terms how she felt as the bike rider came at her from behind and brushed by her, so close that it gave her a bad scare.

She then went on to state her age (mid-seventies), a valid reason for her strong feelings that bicycle riding should be forbidden on the town's busy downtown sidewalks. She pointed out that older people couldn't move as fast as they once did, and that their vision and hearing are often impaired. A fall could be a catastrophe to someone in the older years.

Her premise was sound and stated in reasonable terms. She concluded her piece by reminding readers that sidewalks were for foot traffic.

Anger is not the only emotion to curb when you write an article in which you express your opinions. Avoid a whiney, complaining tone—it turns people off. Present your facts in a straightforward manner and offer a possible solution. A positive and constructive approach gets attention.

Humor is a great device to use when writing about people who upset you. As an example, another former student wrote a delightful piece about how upset she was when company from out of town dropped in unannounced and stayed the weekend, altering all her family's plans. As annoyed as she was, she said she wasn't nearly as upset as her parents were years before, when an aunt came for Sunday dinner and didn't leave until twenty years later. The little anecdote relieved the tone of the piece. She then went on to give several good suggestions on how to avoid situations in which guests overstayed their welcome.

LET'S GET SERIOUS

When you've had some experience writing pet peeves or sound-offs, you may want to write a more serious article (or think piece) expressing your opinion on weightier matters than blaring TV sets or roller skates left in the driveway.

When I think of in-depth, academic writing, the names of William Buckley, Jack Anderson, and William Randolph Hearst Jr. come to mind. Their columns deal with problems affecting whole groups of people, even nations, e.g., the population explosion. Any subject related to politics, the economy, social reform, or scientific research makes good material for the in-depth think piece.

Almost any publication can have a think piece listed on its table of contents page. The July-August '84 issue of *The Saturday Evening Post* included a moving essay titled "I Am the American Flag" by Dr. Robert H. Schuller. Fraternal magazines often publish articles written in a somber tone. "Agent Orange, States Act On" is such a piece, written by Joan Maiman for the *Veterans of Foreign Wars* publication. *Highway Patrolman* takes in-depth articles, such as one titled "California D.U.I. Law: Is It Working?" by William L. Roper, a piece about the effectiveness of the new drunk driving law.

Your daily paper carries serious, thought-provoking articles, sandwiching them in between the sensational news items. Essays and columns are good formats for in-depth think articles. Editorial columns are usually of a serious nature and present the message in a straightforward manner. The business page and the family page will often carry think pieces.

In my current paper is a column on "Pro-Family" written

by Jack Anderson. Another serious-type piece is "How the Public Feels about Nuclear War" by Tom Wicker.

These articles are a bit more difficult to write than most of the other types. Writing about complex problems of major proportions requires something more than just sounding off about a personal frustration.

First of all, you need a strong voice of authority and a style that fits the comparatively heavy issues under discussion. This sound of authority can come from your professional expertise in a particular area, or you have done extensive research into the subject. You can make generous use of quotes from people who *are* authorities in the field.

Writing a full-length think piece requires extensive and thorough research to give the solid substance required. This is not written in an hour or two, or even in a few days. Many interviews are a must, to back up your point of view. The piece must be loaded with firm facts and figures.

Before you get into longer articles (1,500 up to 5,000 words), designed to make people think seriously about a weighty problem, practice writing shorter essays first. Writing a few lighter peeve articles will also get you in training for this long run.

Who, *Me*?

Can you write and sell think articles? Of course you can—just as you can write and sell other types of articles discussed in previous chapters. Because of what I've said about the importance of the voice of authority, you may be a bit skeptical, and with reason. Truthfully, it *is* more difficult to write and sell an in-depth piece.

While it's not absolutely mandatory that you be someone with a world-renowned reputation in some chosen field of endeavor, it helps. But if you're deeply concerned about major problems that involve large numbers of people, or if you're knowledgeable on foreign affairs and the national political scene, don't be afraid to express your opinion in written form. I strongly suggest, however, that you be realistic and accept the fact that you have to work your way up. Begin with letters to the editor of your local paper. Submit your opinions to various fraternal and religious publications. Try the college and literary magazines.

You'll have a greater chance of impressing editors at *The New Yorker, Atlantic Monthly, Harper's, Esquire,* and *The Saturday Evening Post* (top markets for think pieces) if you submit a list of publication credits along with your manuscripts.

A Word of Caution

Inexperienced writers often make the mistake of thinking that big words impress the reader. Multisyllable words should be used only when there is no other word that will do. Whatever type of writing you do, keep in mind always that *good* writing is easy-to-understand writing. The more complex the subject, the greater need for simplicity and clarity of style.

You can be scholarly without confusing the reader with unnecessary high-sounding words. Granted, the think piece is written for a different readership from that of the popular-appeal type of article. The latter is written for a huge readership representing a wide cross section of backgrounds. Even a select readership in today's world, however, appreciates clarity of thought. The words should never come between you and your reader—in any kind of writing.

WHAT'S SO FUNNY?

To my way of thinking, humor is like sex appeal; you either have it or you don't. And if you have "it," who can define this fragile, very special talent?

A scientist or a medical expert can tell us the chemical content of tears, but does that say anything about the emotion that produces the tears? We know what happens when we smile, chuckle, laugh, but can we put into words exactly what it was that we found so funny?

To me, humor is a way of looking at life and seeing the funny side—in almost any situation. People who have this very special, inimitable viewfinder are loved and wanted. They draw us close to them because they "light up life."

Comedians who make us laugh are a priceless part of life. Who could ever fully repay a Jack Benny, a Milton Berle, or a George Burns for the hours and hours of relief they've given us from our daily problems through their ability to make us laugh? With few exceptions, behind the comedian is an unseen figure—the writer, feverishly creating the funny lines to be delivered on stage, at the microphone, or before the camera by the other half of the team. It usually takes both kinds of talent, the ability to deliver the lines and the talent to write the lines, to make a show. Most comedians at one time or another publicly thank their writers for their contributions to the success of a show or program. A second's recognition is all the writer gets from the audience, but writers who create comedy for radio, television, or the stage earn top dollar.

The comedy writer is only one kind of humorist. There are many others. Many start out as a columnist on a small local paper, as did Erma Bombeck. She began her writing career with her hometown paper and ultimately gained world-wide fame as a syndicated columnist. There's Andy Rooney, whose droll humor makes us smile or laugh as we scan his column over our coffee cups. We all have our favorites.

Satire is a delightful form of humor, and you'll find this type in *The New Yorker* and *Esquire.* Whereas the Erma Bombecks deliberately use exaggeration to make their point, the satirist uses a very subtle approach in the form of irony or sarcasm to prick the balloons of our foibles and stupidities.

There is the quaint, colloquial kind of humor that we associate with the well-remembered humorists, Mark Twain and Will Rogers. Those two were past masters at commenting on a human flaw or situation that needed correcting. Lincoln, too, used droll anecdotes to make his points. His was a dry, country-boy humor to which people in all walks of life related.

Whatever the kinds of humor, whether highbrow or lowbrow, there are certain similarities that bond them. The prime purpose of any humor article is to make the reader smile or laugh. But beyond the smile and the chuckle in the humor piece can be a subtle message or point.

You can use humor as a vehicle in any of the seven other article types, of course. Humor skillfully used always softens and lightens the heavy places in an article. In these other types of articles, adding humor requires as much care as adding spices to a recipe. Too much is bad because it takes away from the primary purpose of the article, which may not be humorous at all.

If people are always smiling and laughing at what you say, or the way you say it, the chances are good you'll be able to *write* humor. Keep in mind, however, that you don't have gestures, expressions, and tone of voice to help you along.

Making People Laugh

If you're a new writer and you want to try to write humor, anecdotes are a good place to start. Use your family, your dentist, your doctor, your tax consultant and others who play a role in your life. After you've written a few short anecdotes, if you get any editorial encouragement, go on to longer articles.

Set the humorous tone of your article in the opening lines. Your lead must imply a funny situation to come. As an example, this is the way Erma Bombeck began her column in my morning paper:

> If there is one thing I can't stand, it's being accused of being a sexist . . . especially when the accuser has a point.
>
> A few columns back, I pointed out the need for a greeting card inviting the dawdling husbands to dinner. I think I said there is something Pavlovian about the word "DIIIINAAAAAH!"

Erma goes on to relate how men scurry to clean out the medicine chest, trim their toenails, and set the garbage cans out at the curb . . . just as dinner is announced.

We all relate to whatever Erma Bombeck writes because she uses everyday domestic situations and her family. Her exaggeration, her droll humor, her talent for seeing something funny in every situation, make us smile or laugh right out loud.

All good humor writers use situations readers can identify with—funny sayings of children, anecdotes about other relatives, humorous situations in social gatherings, the military, or politics. Whatever they write about, we, the readers, feel we've been there, or we know someone who has.

Another device used by the humorist is to set himself up as a bumbler—the Rodney Dangerfield approach. This device creates instant reader sympathy, meaning the reader is *with you.* You begin by laughing at yourself, and soon the reader is laughing right along with you.

Don't try to cover the whole world. Pick one facet of a subject, one very funny incident to illustrate your point. As an example, if you're writing about the cute, hilarious thing your three-year-old said, don't try also to include something funny that Aunt Mathilda said. Save Aunt Mathilda for another piece.

Because it's difficult to sustain an emotion like humor, a humorous article should be brief. After the punch line is delivered, get off stage. If you've ever listened to a long-winded friend tell a supposedly funny story, running on and on before getting to the point, you know what I mean. A good length for humor writing is from a *few* lines, as in humorous anecdotes, to a full-length article of 1,000 to 1,500 words.

When something funny hits you, make a note of it in your notebook. Decide the form in which you'll put the incident— filler, anecdote, column, mini article. Then start writing.

As in all types of writing, the words on paper must be chosen with care so as to create the reader response you want. You may have to write the piece several times until you have it honed so that the smile begins on the reader's face with the first sentence, spreads wider with the second paragraph, and then erupts into a laugh at the point where you deliver your punch line.

Test your material on your defenseless family, or on your friends—reading what you wrote aloud. If you get a big smile, a chuckle, or a belly laugh, you'll know you have what it takes to crack this specialized market.

Who'll Buy My Chestnuts?

It's almost impossible to pick up a magazine or a newspaper that doesn't have humorous pieces included in the table of contents. Specialized magazines, for instance publications with the needs of special groups like military wives, or businessmen, or mothers of small children, all carry humor slanted toward their readerships.

Also look at the humor section of your *Writer's Market,* the guide to good marketing, and you'll find listings for magazines devoted solely to humor.

Good humor writing is hard to come by. Editors comb through manuscripts looking for that indefinable something that brings a smile. Yours could be that one manuscript that does it. You'll never know—unless you try.

This chapter on humor and think pieces concludes our discussion on how to write and sell the eight easiest article types. As an extra bonus, the next chapter will show you how to write and sell the *mini* article, short pieces that include fillers, columns, and articles up to approximately 800 words.

I will also share some vitally important information on how to market your articles to best advantage, as well as give you pointers on how to run your writing business in a profitable way. Finally, I'll share with you some very personal thoughts about what it means to be a writer.

The following checklists will help you review the key points made in this chapter.

CHECKLIST FOR PET PEEVES

☑Are you keeping a running account of the situations in life that annoy you? (We each have our own pet peeves. What annoys you might not upset me, and vice versa.)

☑Did you cool down over your pet peeve *before* you tried to write about it?

☑Did you use a touch of humor to lighten the situation?

☑Did you start your peeve with a strong lead that sets the scene, the how and where of the incident?

☑Did you make your point and get off stage?

☑Did you give a constructive solution to eliminate the behavior or situation that caused you to sound off?

CHECKLIST FOR SERIOUS THINK ARTICLES

☑Do you like to read serious pieces by William Buckley, Jack Anderson, William Randolph Hearst Jr., and others who write on political, social, and economic problems?

☑Do you have a strong voice of authority and a style that fits the serious tone and character required by this type of piece?

☑Have you taken the time to research your subject thoroughly to back up your point of view?

☑Does the situation or problem about which you wrote concern enough readers to interest a publisher in your article?

☑Do you avoid high-sounding words in the interests of clarity?

☑Do you offer concrete suggestions or sound philosophical thoughts on the problem discussed in your think piece?

☑Will what you have to say really make people think and take action?

CHECKLIST FOR HUMOR PIECES

☑Do you see the "funny" side of life? (Every situation has its comical aspect.)

☑Do you make a point to listen to the great humorists of our times, as for example, George Burns, Joan Rivers, Rodney Dangerfield, and Rich Little, or any other of *your* favorites? Do you note how and where they get their laughs in their monologues?

☑Do you read and clip columns and pieces written by Erma Bombeck, Andy Rooney, Art Hoppe, and other contemporary humorists? Do you keep notes about their style that would help you write humor?

☑Do you read the great humorists of the past, such as Mark Twain, Will Rogers, Abraham Lincoln, and even Shakespeare?

☑Do you study the cartoons in your favorite magazines and newspapers and clip the ones you like? Do you read Post Scripts in *The Saturday Evening Post?* Satire pieces in *The New Yorker?*

☑Is *your* humorous piece really funny? Have you tried it out on friends and family? Did they smile or laugh?

☑Did you keep your "funny" story brief?

☑Did you revise and polish your humor piece as you would any other type of article?

☑Does your lead set the humorous tone?

☑Does your humor article hurt anyone? It shouldn't.

When Less Is More—
Writing Mini Articles
and Columns

M any writers find a good market for their ideas through writing mini articles—short fillers and featurette pieces that run anywhere from 300 to under 1,000 words—and short columns (about 750 words). Most magazines and newspapers are always in need of short items that can be fitted into bits of space left over after the full-length articles have been placed, and most have regular columns by one writer.

MINIS—TO MAKE A LONG STORY SHORT

In addition to allowing flexibility in page makeup, short articles and fillers lend additional interest to the content of a page. Shakespeare said, "Brevity is the soul of wit." Good advice to the humorist. Brevity is also the soul of successful publishing when it comes to mini articles.

But brevity is not the only requirement a mini must meet in order to be published. As there is a format and technique to the longer article types discussed in previous chapters, so there is a definite structure for fillers and short articles.

Whether your mini piece is a short filler of only 300 words, or a very short article of 1,000 words, it must give the reader a take-away. These pieces have a purpose—they can entertain, inform, or inspire. In order to succeed in the take-away, the short piece should focus on one small aspect of a subject; there isn't the space to explore it in depth. It's one sharp bird's-eye glimpse of a topic that you give the reader, not a leisurely, lingering view.

Mini articles fall into several classifications, as for example, short columns, amusing anecdotes, so-called Op-Ed pieces (opinion-editorial comments), and fillers from one-liners, such as cute sayings of children, pithy quotations from the known and unknown, and any idea you can write in 300 words or fewer.

If you're interested in writing fillers, I recommend two books on the subject: *How to Make Money Writing Little Articles, Anecdotes, Hints, Recipes, Light Verse and Other Fillers* by Connie Emerson, and *How to Write Fillers* by Louise

Boggess. Connie Emerson's book was published in 1983 by Writer's Digest Books. Louise Boggess's was the first book on the subject and was published by Funk & Wagnalls, first printing, 1968. You'll find more on these books in the Bibliography.

MAKE IT SNAPPY

Many new writers think that writing a short article or story is easier than writing a longer piece. Such is not the case. Mistakes that are made in longer works can sometimes be forgiven if the overall writing is excellent. As an example, in a long 150,000-word historical novel or book, there might be occasional passages that some readers would consider dull, and readers have been known to admit that they "skipped over some pages," hurrying on to the more exciting sections where dialogue and action quickened the pace.

In contrast, when you have a few hundred words in which to tell a story, every single word counts. There can be no dull places. The dramatic impact, the emotional satisfaction for the reader, must come fast in any mini article. You haven't the words for a slow buildup of reader interest; it has to be there from the beginning.

In writing short articles and fillers, think of yourself as saying goodbye to a friend at the train depot. He's on the train, which is already moving. You have only a moment to impart one last *important* piece of information. Under these circumstances, it's amazing what you could say in a very few words. There'd be no chit-chatting. You'd get right to the point.

"See you in Denver at the family reunion. Don't forget. Christmas Eve!" That might be the bare bones of the message. As Jack Webb used to say on his memorable *Dragnet* series, "Just the facts, Ma'am."

Guaranteed to Shrink

Brevity *is* the soul of fillers and short articles. Paragraphs should be short, crisp, yet pungent. Readers must be able to recognize the point of the piece immediately. There's not the wordage to say, in effect, "Let's look at it another way."

To attain a clear, sharp style, keep your sentences simple. Avoid long, compound constructions such as, "And thus we see that," or "As has been said before. . . ." One word must do the work of several. Strong, active verbs and distinctive nouns help to create vivid pictures in the reader's mind and give quick pacing.

Use adjectives and adverbs sparingly. Replace *he was walking slowly* with, He *strolled* or he *ambled* or he *sauntered.* It takes practice to "write tight," as my newspaper editor, Bill Drake, used to call it when the paper had fewer pages because the advertising for that week had fallen off. "Write tight" means you go through your copy with a blue pencil and line out every unnecessary word. Another way to tighten your writing is to take a long paragraph ana divide it in two, using only *one* part.

If you find that what you intended as a short article runs long in spite of an all-out effort to tighten and shorten, consider that the subject you chose may not be suitable for a mini article but may require full-article treatment.

Before the reader can catch that sharp bird's-eye view I mentioned earlier, you, the writer, must first narrow your viewfinder, "iris in," as it's sometimes called.

Write Tight

John Bryan, a prolific contributor of mini articles to a wide assortment of sports magazines, in addition to producing a weekly fishing column for twelve newspapers, says he gets his bird's-eye view of a subject by first writing his idea out on a sheet of paper. He then spends the next five minutes listing everything his article might include. He looks over the list until he sees something that might fit a specific theme.

In an article published in the August '84 edition of *Writer's Digest,* Bryan describes in detail how he wrote a humorous "shortie" on the subject of theme parks.

First, he wrote down his general topic—*theme parks.* Second, he listed Walt Disney World; fishing at Six Flags; roller coasters; lakes; free fishing lures; live entertainment; free tickets for fish.

Out of this exercise came the exact theme he would use in his 500-word article, a *new* theme park, which he called "Five Fish Over Frisco."

Bryan says his next decision was to settle on what he could include within such a short article, as well as the best format, or treatment. Bryan wrote in his *Writer's Digest* article:

> I decided a *survey* article would be best. A quick survey would give the reader a brief summary of the park's theme areas.

In his summary of places not to be missed Bryan listed:

Crappieland
Catfish County
Bluegill Boulevard
Sucker City
Trout Territory

He briefly mentioned food items, such as Carp Crepes and Mullet on a Stick. In his 500 words he was also able to include a short listing of several fun rides, such as Catfish Coaster, Haunted Halibut, and Minnow-Go-Round. "Five Fish over Frisco" appeared in half a dozen newspapers.

MARKETING THE MINI

There's a year-round need for mini pieces to fill up unused space in magazines and newspapers. Except for seasonal or holiday items, there's no need to submit your minis weeks or months ahead. The editor will use your material whenever and wherever the need arises. It's not even necessary to query the editor. Often the mini is added at the last minute to fill a "hole" in a page.

Look through your favorite magazines and newspapers and you'll be surprised at the number of fillers and short articles that appear. Here are a few examples from magazines you're undoubtedly familiar with, and you may even subscribe to a few.

Guideposts wants short manuscripts, approximately 250-750 words, for such features as "Quiet People." Their editorial guidelines state, "A writer would have the best chance to submit a 1-page or 2-page article—very short."

Catholic Digest says it wants fillers: Jokes, anecdotes, and short humor—10-300 words.

Scope (Lutheran publication) wants "Interesting, brief, pithy, significant, or clever filler items."

Good Housekeeping wants housekeeping fillers, humorous material, jokes, anecdotes, and ideas for "The Better Way."

Ladycom, the magazine for wives of military men, wants short material for columns and "It Seems to Me" section. Subjects—travel, experiences of life lived at various bases, posts and nearby cities, "Your Pet," "BabyCom." 1,000 to 1,800 words.

Redbook wants material for "Young Mother's Story." Length from 1,500 words (a little longer mini than most.) Also accepts short articles of 1,000 words.

Woman's Day uses fillers for "Neighbors" and "Tips to Share" columns. Pays for each practical suggestion on homemaking, child rearing and relationships.

Saturday Evening Post—Columns and Departments are: Editorials, Food, Medical Mailbox, Religious Columns, Travel, and Fillers (pays per gag, anecdote, postscript, or short humor piece).

Parade wants short articles 800 to 1,500 words.

Reader's Digest uses a variety of short material for "Life in These United States," "Campus Comedy," and many other short features.

These are just a few of the many markets you'll find for fillers and short articles listed in your *Writer's Market* and *Writer's Handbook.* Take an hour or so on a day when perhaps the creative juices are not flowing and browse through your market guides. You'll be amazed. You're sure to come up with an idea that will fit snugly into some column, department, or special feature of some publication.

Don't overlook your special-subject publications. *Travel-Holiday,* for instance, uses featurettes on small towns, cities, museums, markets, shopping sites, art galleries, and other similar subjects of interest to the traveler. Another wide-open market for short material is the confession market, each one of the magazines featuring short material in their various advice, medical, psychological, and homemaking sections.

Mini Spinoffs

Mini article spin-offs surface when, for one reason or another, a long article doesn't sell. Often by condensing the reject into two or three mini articles, you can spin off your subject matter into several shortie article sales.

Keeping in mind the importance of slanting can provide you with spin-offs. For instance, suppose you had found a nifty new way to pack more into your carry-on bag for a short weekend flight. You don't want to bother with other luggage that would end up on the carousel in the baggage claim department, with possibly a long wait.

This idea could be a helpful filler item, perhaps titled, "How To Pack More into Less." To target your markets, as in any type of article, you would consider the *needs* of the reader—several kinds of readers. The college student anticipating a weekend home or on the ski slopes would have far different needs from those of the military wife with a young baby en route to join her husband for a weekend. The retired couple joyously looking forward to a weekend with son or daughter would have still different needs, but there is one common denominator: the need to get as much as possible crammed into that one carry-on bag. So you slant your idea to several markets, keeping in mind the *must-takes* for each type of reader. The focus of the filler or mini article in each submission would be on the *how* of packing that one carry-on.

ABOUT COLUMNS

Many writers have begun their writing careers with columns written for their local papers. *Column* implies continuous appearance in a newspaper or other periodical. Some have gone on to fame in the writing profession by having their columns *syndicated* (the column sells to a newspaper corporation or chain, such as Hearst or Scripps-Howard Syndicates, who then publish it in any number of their newspapers). The modest pay previously received from just one sale to a local paper, with syndication is multiplied into many checks from numerous newspapers and Sunday supplements.

When we think of syndication, we think of the popular advice columns that are read in millions of homes throughout the country simultaneously, over the morning cup of coffee or after the children are tucked away in bed. Other types of syndicated columns come from William Buckley, Art Buchwald, Erma Bombeck, Joe Carcione, the Green Grocer, Russell Baker (New York Times Service), and many others undoubtedly familiar to you. All of these famous columnists have one thing in common, a fact that should be inspiring to you: They *all* started out in their local paper.

Erma Bombeck, whose smiling face made the cover of *Time* magazine (July 2, 1984), an accomplishment considered to be the epitome of success, started out in Centerville, Ohio, in the early sixties writing for her hometown paper. Now her column is syndicated in 900 papers in the U.S. and Canada, and she's a frequent guest on such programs as *Good Morning America,* on ABC TV.

You have just as good a chance to see your face on a future edition of *Time* magazine as Erma, provided you can give members of the reading public a column that tickles their funny bone à la Bombeck, makes them think as William Buckley does, or provides them with acceptable answers for such age-old problems as adolescent acne or the upheaval caused by visiting in-laws—the answers given by such pros as Ann Landers, Dear Abby, and Helen Bottel.

Several of my students have courageously launched their careers as columnists. Eileen Walter, a Writer's Digest School student who lives at a place with the enchanting name of Falling Star Farm, Hewitt, Minnesota, wrote her first column in 1981 with the lovely title of "Catch a Falling Star," a column published in the *Wadena Pioneer Journal.* The column led to writing feature articles, Eileen wrote me, and to being editor of the "People" page of her daily paper. Eileen says:

> I find that the experience of living helps me project emotion into my nonfiction. I've been in places and situations you wouldn't believe, and held every kind of job. I write from these experiences in my column.

Eileen's advice to new writers goes like this:

> Let your emotion get out onto the paper. Don't let well-meaning nonwriters read your material and give "helpful" advice. Open up all five senses and "feel" the world through them each day. Even if you're bored, see, feel, and file it all away for future reference. Later, when you least expect it, something you filed away will be helpful in what you're writing, supplying you with a subject for your article or column.

Eileen's sensitivity to the world she sees at Falling Star Farm is reflected in her columns and in her short articles. Her advice is excellent.

Daci Boring, a former student in one of my adult education classes, writes a column headed "About People" for her local paper, *The Vallejo Independent Press.* When I sent her a questionnaire seeking information on her beginnings as a columnist, this is what she said:

> I imagine I first sold myself as a writer with something to say when I approached the local newspaper and said I had a column idea and would like to write for the paper. I had read where the present columnist was taking a sabbatical, time off

for awhile, and so I hot-footed it down to the paper. I talked my way into doing a weekly column for the *impressive* sum of $10.00 for each column used.

In my first column, I wrote about my meeting with a juvenile whale shark. I used my experience as a SCUBA diver to write the story. The second column was based on my observations of handicapped people. I used my knowledge of human nature for that one.

Daci writes about people the way *she* sees them. One of her later columns is titled, "Is That All There Is?," a column about Jean Richards, a professional hypnotist. Her column on the handicapped reflected the poignancy of the subject matter and was titled, appropriately enough, "Appreciating 'Little Things' Like Seeing and Running."

Ethel Bangert, a long-time writer friend, does a now-syndicated column titled, "Collectibles Corner." Ethel is a versatile writer, author of thirty novels and over 600 articles. For over forty years she has held the line through the ups and downs that characterize the writing profession, and for her great productivity was awarded the Golden Heart Award by the Romance Writers of America at their 1984 convention.

In answer to my questionnaire, Ethel wrote:

I travel a great deal and I collect material everywhere I go. I also study. I recently took classes on antiques at the Winterthur Museum in Delaware—at $100.00 per day. Very costly, but when you want knowledge you're willing to pay for it, and what I gleaned from the classes helped my column, "Collectibles Corner." I feel the column on collectibles is more up to date and packed with more solid information from what I learned in those classes.

My advice to new writers is simply, *hang in there.* You'll have days, weeks, and months of discouragement, but no one twisted your arm to force you to write. It was *your* choice and this is "grown-up work," a lifetime job. You have to be tough enough to take the disappointments. Your words are not gospel, but they could be turned into pure gold.

To convince an editor that you have the staying power to "hang in there," it's wise to write at least a dozen columns to present in your initial interview. Any writer can turn out a clever, witty, pithy column or two (well, *nearly* every writer), but what about a deadline that stares you in the face day after day, perhaps 300 or more times a year? What gives this staying power to writers like the pros I have mentioned and some newcomers such as the students I have quoted?

For twenty-five years Helen Bottel authored her column, "Helen Help Us." Recently she was approached by a Japanese paper to write an advice column strictly for Japanese readers. When interviewed on this exciting global widening of her readership, Helen admitted she knew very little about Japanese culture and tradition. For the past twenty years, she'd lived in Sacramento, California, and had only spent one night in Japan, on a stopover visit.

This being a stranger to much of Japanese life didn't bother the editor of *Yomiuri Shimbun*, the leading newspaper in Japan with the largest newspaper circulation in the world. What did interest the Japanese editor was Helen's empathy with all kinds of people, as well as her humor and her straightforward philosophy. Also, Helen's columns reflect the American viewpoint on family relationships and problems, something the Japanese find most interesting.

Helen Bottel's recognition as a columnist who can break through the culture barrier, reaching into homes in a land far away from her own, points up the traits that are inherent in all lasting columnists—empathy with and sympathy for other people, and a strong desire to help or to inform.

To succeed, a column must have one hallmark—the indelible stamp of the author, a style and voice unlike any other. It's your unique way of looking at life and your way of presenting what you see that will win editorial acceptance. Your column idea should also be focused on one area or one arena of human behavior. Erma Bombeck's focus, right from the beginning and continuing without a break, is

> Housework, if it is done right, can kill you. Women who kept house in the happy hunting ground called suburbia were so lonely that they held meaningful conversations with their tropical fish . . . You become about as exciting as your food blender. The kids come in, look you in the eye, and ask you if anybody is home.

Said with deliciously fey humor, but making a point. According to the *Time* magazine profile on Erma, the message this columnist sends hasn't changed in twenty years. The women she wrote for at first have gone on to "divorces, master's degrees and careers," but they still read Erma Bombeck, chuckle, smile, nod their heads and think, "That's so true!"

If you think you have the uniqueness and the staying power, then go for it and put together a dozen columns, each one focusing on *one* side of life as we humans know it. "Hot-foot it" down to your local paper, talk to the editor, as Daci Boring and all the others did at one time. Your chances are just as good as theirs were.

You'll never become another Bombeck, another Buckley, another Bangert, or Boring. There can be only one of each of them. But what you can do is create your own image. The more individualistic you are, the better your chances will be to fill that column space in some newspaper. An editor, and ultimately his readership, can spot this individuality in a minute if it's where it should be, in the opening paragraph.

Consider the opening of a "Collectibles Corner" column Ethel Bangert wrote on *button collecting*.

> The cells were named the "dim and darks." And dark they were, for when I stepped into one a pitch blackness surrounded me. These were the dreaded cells used for tough men in the early years in Tasmania, Australia. Some of the prisoners, to keep from going mad, threw the buttons from their "general issue" uniforms around the cells and then crawled around trying to find them again. When the guards discovered this, they took the buttons away.

> For some reason, buttons have often played strange roles in human drama.

Ethel then goes on in her column to tell stories about the many parts buttons have played in human drama down through history. She ends her column by circling back to her lead:

> If buttons interest you, try to find some unusual metal ones, perhaps once a part of a uniform proudly worn in armory drill or on the parade ground instead of in battle. Or, even the poor things that once were part of "general issue" for men of the "dim and darks."

Columns Mean Commitment

At one point in my writing career, I originated a continuing column for my local weekly paper, *The Pacifica Tribune.* The column was to be of the "people" type in which local names made news—anything I thought would interest the over-the-coffee-cup readers in our coastal town. My editor, Bill Drake, left it up to me to name the column. After many tries, I came up with the heading, "Social Tides," capitalizing on the lovely geographical setting beside the Pacific Ocean.

As the weeks and months flew by, "Social Tides" became almost a living personality. Friends and neighbors stopped me on the street with, "I've got a juicy tidbit for 'Social Tides.' " Readers wrote in to the paper saying how much they enjoyed reading the items. The column was a source of great personal pleasure to me, a place where I could more or less let my hair down and do my own thing—as long as I remembered to focus on my main theme—what people were doing in our town.

The weekly column gave me a discipline that has served me all my writing life. I *know* the importance of deadlines. By writing the column weekly, no matter how I felt or what domestic upheavals occurred, I learned that for every time you write from pure inspiration there are a dozen times you write because someone is depending on you. You've made a commitment and you must honor it.

This sense of commitment applies to all writing, or should, but in writing columns you're faced with daily or weekly deadlines rather than some vague far-off one that depends on making the sale, or getting the contract.

If you do decide to write a column, be aware that you are committing yourself to what Ethel Bangert called, "Adult Work"—a job that must be done come hell or high water.

SHORT IS SWEET

To summarize, try writing short instead of long. You'll find it a welcome change of pace if you're into some major horrendous writing project. If you can't quite decide whether you're ready for a full-length article project, a filler or mini article might trigger inspiration for a more in-depth piece later. If you're just beginning your writing career, one of the best ways in which you can break into publication is through writing fillers, featurettes, or one of the other mini types I listed earlier.

Or could you be ready for a column? While the monetary rewards might be great, as in the case of the syndicated columnists, for most columnists who fill space mostly in their local paper—at least, for a long time—the rewards come in such things as personal pride and satisfaction. A column appearing regularly can be the ego boost you need, perhaps at a difficult time in your writing career.

There's a special joy that comes with knowing the whole town is reading you at the breakfast table, or dinner table, and a thrill that never quite melts away when someone says, "I read your column last night. I sure enjoyed it."

Writing a 750-word column could be the beginning of all sorts of good things for you. It's certainly worth a try.

CHECKLIST FOR MINI ARTICLES

☑Have you written "tight"? Have you made every word count?

☑Have you created instant word pictures by using *active* verbs and *striking* nouns? Have you avoided excess-baggage adjectives and adverbs?

☑Have you focused on one small facet of a subject and avoided trying to tell all in one mini piece?

☑Have you caught the reader's attention before the train pulls out? Remember the goodbye at the depot?

☑If your mini article does have a seasonal or holiday tie-in, have you submitted it far enough in advance of the special issue date?

☑Are you keeping a list of possible mini ideas so that you have a good inventory from which to draw when perhaps the well runs dry on longer (full-length) articles?

From Telling to Selling— Selling— How to Market Your Articles

The preceding chapters have been all about how to write the most popular types of articles appearing in magazines and newspapers month after month. By now you've probably decided on the kinds of articles you want to write. Your notebook is filling up with ideas and you can't wait to get started—if you haven't started already.

You may have articles out to market and you're watching for the mailman, hoping he'll bring one of those long, slim envelopes instead of the too-familiar manuscript size. I'm keeping my fingers crossed for you to get the letter saying, "We like your article and we want to publish it." If you shouldn't be so fortunate this time, help is on the way. This chapter will fulfill the promise implied in the second part of the title of this book—*how to sell what you write.* What you are about to learn will take much of the guesswork out of trying to find the *right* market for your articles.

The first step in good marketing procedure is to identify the publications that might be interested in your article. This is called *market research,* a procedure enthusiastically endorsed by most professional, selling writers.

RESEARCHING

To thoroughly research a potential publication for your work, you need to study at least a year's worth of back issues. You won't have enough magazines on your subscription list to do the job, so a trip to the library is necessary. At the library you can ask for back issues and settle down in a quiet corner, with your notebook handy. You will study the content of a particular magazine, remembering that *content* means more than just the table of contents.

You'll begin your selection of a particular market (magazine) with one you think might be interested in the subject of your article. For example, an article on the danger of sending children to school too soon would fit nicely into *Parents Magazine.* An article on how to quit smoking would interest *Prevention,* or *Family Health.* An article all about a terrific cruise you took that didn't cost a fortune might go to *Travel-Holiday.*

If you're unsure as to just where your article might fit, it's a good idea to spend some time browsing through *Writer's Market* or *Writer's Handbook,* the yearly marketing guides put out in hard cover by *Writer's Digest* and *The Writer.* These two marketing guidebooks will tell you the kinds of articles wanted by a wide variety of publications.

Settled at the library, begin your close scrutiny of the back issues of one magazine at a time. Notice the covers; you'll find that they give the reader the first clue to the type of subject matter likely to be found in the magazine. The lead article is usually featured on the cover, along with two or three other attention-getting article titles. By *lead* article, I mean that the editor considers this article to be of special interest to the readers. It's a magazine seller.

Because it so clearly demonstrates the importance of a magazine cover, I'll take the September '84 issue of *Travel-Holiday* as an example. The lead article, as indicated by larger print and its position in first place, is titled, "Shanghai—a World Apart." To heighten the interest in the subject matter, the Orient, the "mystique of Shanghai" is evoked by the face of an elderly Chinese man in the cover photograph.

Other cover titles, "The Inns and Outs of New England Foliage," "Autumn with America's Wildlife," "Birth of a Cruise Ship," and "Germany's Food, Wine, and Rhine," tell you that the magazine "Roams the Globe," as its cover slogan proclaims. If your article happened to be on some exotic foreign port, you'd list this magazine as a possibility in the *marketing* section of your notebook.

After a thorough study of the magazine's cover, go to the table of contents page. On this page titles are given with descriptive captions beneath, such as, "Shanghai—A Chinese city with a Western beat"; "Hail to the Leaf"; "On the New England Trail"; and "Birth of a Cruise Ship, Born to a Life of Leisure."

The captions give you the focus of the article and set the mood. The table of contents page also tells you who wrote the article. Make a note of the names of writers who have published repeatedly in a certain magazine. These authors make good models for less experienced writers.

A study of titles will give you an idea of the *balance* of a magazine, that is, how many profiles, how-tos, personal experience articles, etc. are used in a given issue.

After studying the cover and the table of contents page, you're ready for the next step, reading the editorials, including the editor's column if there is one. This will give you clues to how an editor views his readership. Keep in mind that editors' most important task is finding the kinds of articles their readers want to read.

Other indications of readership interests are reflected in the special departments, features, letters to the editor and various columns. Studying the special sections of a magazine will help you find the right market for your article—a magazine with readers interested in what *you* wrote about.

The next item for consideration in your market research is a study of the blurbs, those sentences usually appearing between the title and the beginning of the article.

Blurbs are teasers, like window displays that draw the customer into the store to buy. The customer in this case is the reader, and the blurb whets his interest in what the article has to say about a given subject. In writing the blurb, the editor takes an exciting element in the article and uses that as "window display." When you write the final draft of your article, it's a good idea to think in terms of the blurb the editor might write to showcase your piece. Make sure you have something exciting that would make a good blurb.

Next on your list for study are the illustrations or photographs which catch the reader's attention, and also have captions printed beside or below them to highlight the significance of the illustration.

Now that you have an overall picture in your mind of the character or personality of a given magazine, you're ready to study the articles themselves.

Remember the discussion of building blocks in Chapter One? In feeling out the kind of writing an editor wants in his magazine, start with block number one, *the lead.* What type of lead was used? Was it a description lead, the type you often find as a beginning for travel articles? A direct quote from someone you'll meet later in the article? A startling statement or attention-getting statistic? If the magazine is not library property, you can use the margin to indicate the type of lead, marking it with a highlighter pencil. If you're browsing through library magazines, make a note in your notebook of each article you study as you go along.

You might even copy a lead that appealed to you, for later study. Collecting good article leads is one of the best ways I know for you to learn to write salable copy. The lead in an article is like a narrative hook in a short story. The purpose of both is to grab readers by the collar, get their attention away from other distractions, and make them want to read on. In studying published articles, you have examples of leads that worked. The editors bought the articles because right from the beginning the pieces caught and held their attention.

From your own magazines at home, you can clip articles you think are good models, make up file folders by type of article, and so keep the clipped pieces for future referral.

When you're familiar with the kinds of leads used by a particular magazine, go on to the other building blocks—the premise, the body, the transitions, the conclusion, and the theme. You might like to use different colored pencils or pens to distinguish one element from another. You may have your own system for highlighting material you want to go over again at a later time.

There is one final clue to the type of material used in a certain publication, an element you might overlook. I'm talking about the *advertisements*. Advertisers pay a large part of the cost of publishing a magazine or newspaper. The number of articles and short stories that appear in an issue are dependent upon a good supply of advertisements.

Because the advertising dollar is so important to the survival of a magazine or a newspaper, editors naturally are reluctant to take any article that might offend any of their advertisers. As an example, a magazine running advertisements for expensive natural furs such as sealskin coats would hardly carry an article blasting away at the cruelty of fur trappers. A strong antidrinking article would hardly fit into a publication that carries jet set liquor ads.

DOES YOUR ARTICLE FIT?

Once you've analyzed a magazine, studying a year's back issues, you're ready to think about where *your* article idea might be appropriate. The following is a list of questions you can ask yourself before you write your article. The time spent in this before-writing exercise will save you the disappointment of a rejection later because you sent your article to the wrong market.

Before you actually write your article, it's a good idea to apply the study or *market research* technique to several magazines or newspapers that are directed to the same type of readership. Studying more than one publication gives you several markets where you might target your article.

1. In studying a year's issues of a magazine, how long has it been since the subject matter of your article appeared? Usually, editors don't like to take articles on the same subject (unless a completely fresh twist is used) more often than once every two years.

2. In what way will your article help the reader, inform him, entertain him, or inspire him? What is the specific purpose of your article? What reader need does it meet?

3. Does your idea conflict with an editorial policy that reflects reader feelings? For instance, *Ranger Rick* magazine will not run articles on pet possums because the philosophy of the publication is against having wild animals as pets.

4. Does your *style* of writing fit the style of the magazine or newspaper markets you've chosen? There is as much difference in the style of writing in various publications as there is difference in style of automobiles built by different companies. The manufacturers, foreign and domestic, cater to different types of buyers. It's just as important for your style to match the tastes of your buyer, the reader.

5. Will the word length suggested by the already published

articles, and by *Writer's Market,* be the right length for your article? Can you complete your idea in the required wordage? Think seriously about word length because nothing will get you a rejection quicker than sending a 3,000-word article to a market whose limit is 1,500 words.

6. From studying a particular magazine, or several in the same category, do you see a pattern in the types of articles the editor prefers? Can you adapt your subject matter to one of the types?

If you can give a yes, a positive answer, to these questions, you're well on your way to writing an article that will have good sales potential. You know from your careful market research that your article will interest the readership of several magazines or newspapers. Now all you have to do is convince the editors. This is where the query letter plays an important part in your success.

THE QUERY LETTER

As a nonfiction writer, you'll find the query letter one of the best tools you'll ever use in carving out a place for yourself in the world of publication. It's your calling card. It's your introduction to the editor. It's your sales pitch, your advance guard. It's the first and most important step you take in submitting your article to an editor.

Writing a good query letter requires the same writing talent and care required by the article itself. This is not the place to "dash off" a hurried note to the editor. The query reflects your style of writing and establishes your credibility as a writer who can produce the proposed article.

Query Guidelines

There are several guidelines to help you with this part of your job.

1. Keep your letter short. Usually one page is enough to convince an editor you have something exciting to send. You should be able to pack what you want to say into four to six

short paragraphs. Each paragraph performs a certain function.

First paragraph— *The lead* Should grab the editor's attention.

Example: Child abuse has reached shocking proportions. Every two minutes a child somewhere is beaten or sexually assaulted. The next victim could be *your* child.

Second paragraph— *Statement of problem*

Example: In spite of recent publicity on child abuse, too many people are sticking their heads in the sand, parents included, refusing to see the danger. What can be done to awaken public awareness to this social tragedy? Can anything be done?

Third paragraph— *Solutions* The article's premise.

Example: Fortunately, something *is* being done. Such groups as [names of organizations devoted to solving the problem] are . . . . [A quote or two from authorities, police, child psychologists, etc., showing how concerned people are working to make others aware of the problem.]

Fourth paragraph— Statements showing how you intend to write your article—the type of article, length, and treatment. Who (readership) will be benefited by reading the article.

Fifth paragraph— Asks, "Would you be interested in my article, 'The Stranger at Your Door—Your Child Could Be the Next Victim.'? If so, I can have the article on your desk by the first of the month."

The most important paragraphs in your query are the first, in which you capture the editor's attention, and the third, in which you give the premise of your article, the point you'll make, and establish your authority. Your authority shines through in the research you've done on the subject—the quotes from leading experts, your case histories, and the facts and figures that support your premise.

2. Opinion is divided among professional writers as to the wisdom of sending out several query letters to a number of editors simultaneously. Some professionals feel that it's unfair to take an editor's time to read your query when at that moment another editor may have sent you an acceptance.

On the other hand, other nonfiction writers feel that timeliness is often of great importance in selling a particular article, and it's perfectly all right to query several editors at the same time, giving the article to the one who responds first.

If you are a beginning writer, my personal feeling is that you should contact one editor at a time. Another suggestion is for you to carefully check the editorial guidelines in *Writer's Market* and *The Writer's Handbook* for how editors feel about multiple query letters. Some editors state outright that they don't want a query letter that has been sent around to other editorial offices. Others say it's all right to multiple query.

3. Always include a stamped, self-addressed envelope with your query letter. Such thoughtfulness is the mark of a professional.

4. Address your query to a specific editor by name. You'll find names of editors on the table of contents page of a magazine, or on the editorial page of a newspaper. You'll also find a listing of editors by name in *Writer's Market* and in *Writer's Handbook.*

Editors move around and change editorial chairs often. Addresses can change overnight. Be on the safe side and check to make sure you have current information. It might tarnish your professional status to send a query letter to an editor who has moved his office into the next world.

5. There are times when you don't query. With certain

types of articles—nostalgia, profiles on people not widely known, humor articles, and mini articles or fillers, it would be difficult for an editor to judge suitability without seeing the completed manuscript.

6. Keep track of all query letters you mail out to editors. Many writers keep the record on index cards. The following is an example of how a query submission card might look.

Query Letter Submissions

Date Mailed	Title	Publication . . . . Editor's Name	Result	Date
10-30-85	Child Abuse 1500 words	Goodhskpng	Rejected "overstocked"	11-23-85
11-24-85	Informative	Parents	Rejected "Too similar "to previous art. Try us again."	12-27-85
1-10-86		Sunday Supplement San Fran Chronicle	Sale $350	1-30-86

The entries on this card are fictional—to show you how you might want to record your queries.

In addition to your index card entries, you might want to make a more detailed record in your notebook. It might be set up as follows:
    Section Labeled—*Query Letters—Out*

- *Title of article* and *length.*
- *Type of article*—(one of the 8)
- *Date query mailed*
- *Name of publication,* with identification, such as men's adventure, women's slick, religious, newspaper, etc.
- *Editor's name and specific title*—senior editor, craft editor, special features editor, etc. Make sure you spell the editor's name correctly.
- *Result.* Date of reply. Type of response—rejection;

"green light," a note from editor saying he'd like to see your article on speculation. Not a sale. Sale. Amount paid for article.

Keeping an accurate record of your query submissions will pay off in several ways. You have proof of your professional status, should the IRS ever audit your tax deductions. It helps you become sensitive to the marketplace because of the editorial comments you record in your notebook. A file box filled with index cards showing you have many query letters going out on different articles is the best motivation I know of for that professional feeling. You're in business, and you have records to prove you are.

The Response

Your query letter can bring several types of answers. They are:

1. A cold rejection slip—cause for momentary despair.
2. A rejection slip with editorial notation such as, "Sorry! Overstocked at the moment." "Too similar to material already bought. Try us again." Cause for a brief pang of disappointment followed by rising hope. "Try us again!" *The editor liked my writing.*
3. Short letter or note—"We're interested in your article idea and would like to see the completed manuscript." (Not a sale—yet) This is what is known among writers as "the green light," an indication that the editor's attention and interest were caught by the subject matter. Your query letter did its job. It was an attention-grabber.
4. Best of all possible worlds—"We'd like to buy your article. Send it to us as soon as possible."

These are the possibilities awaiting you after your query letter is mailed. Each one is important in its own way. Even that cold rejection slip. A turndown on a query doesn't mean necessarily that you're a rotten writer and you should think of taking up some other occupation—such as panning for gold. Query letters are received in all editorial offices in overwhelming numbers. Often editorial staffs are small and personnel are not available to write individual notes to writers explaining why an article idea was turned down. The reasons for rejection could be due to inventory—too many articles on hand already; your article idea was too similar to one recently published or scheduled for publication; your style and format don't quite conform to those required by the publication; the writing was not professional enough to warrant publication.

Staring dolefully at a rejection slip, you'll never know exactly why you received it. You can console yourself by supposing the reason for rejection to be one of the less cruel ones.

A rejection slip with even one word, "Sorry!" scribbled on it is reason for hope. Editors and those who help them don't have time for meaningless notations. A *sorry* means just that. Someone saw something good in your idea and really regretted not being able to send you an acceptance letter. If you get one of these encouraging little notations, take heart. The next editor might see even more in your work.

If you get a letter asking you to send your completed manuscript, again it's important to make your final draft as salable as possible. If your final draft isn't ready as yet, acknowledge the "green light, go-ahead" letter with a warm thank-you and state the date you will submit. Having set a definite date for submission, keep your promise at all costs.

Submitting the Manuscript

Always include a self-addressed, manuscript-size envelope with sufficient postage affixed to cover the return of your article if necessary.

Don't be cute and turn pages upside down to flag you that the manuscript wasn't read past page 5. Don't do your own illustrations or submit your own photographs unless you have a go-ahead from the editor.

Be aware that the green light could still turn to red. After reading your completed article, for any number of reasons the editor might still reject it. Having reached this point, the editor will most likely write you a letter telling you why the publication can't use the article after all. If this happens, send the article on to the next editor—after making any revisions that might improve the piece.

If you get a letter of acceptance, you know what to do. Go out and celebrate! Then write the editor a short letter thanking him for his interest in your work, and if you have another idea you think might interest him, immediately start the query process over again, either in the letter itself or in an accompanying memo.

When you submit your articles, follow the same method of recording submission activity as you used for your query letters. Know where your article is at all times and how long it's been out.

The Waiting Game

How long should you wait? The listings in the *Writer's Market* and in *Writers' Handbook* often tell you how long it takes a certain publication to reply. While you don't want to make a pest of yourself, I feel it is all right to pick up the telephone and call the editorial office if you don't hear within two to three weeks after the designated date as given in the market guides.

Most editors make a reply to a manuscript submission in the nonfiction field within six weeks to two months. If your article has an urgent timeliness, the subject matter being of great current interest, you can indicate in your query letter that you'd appreciate an immediate reply, and flag your manuscript "Subject matter timely. Early reply appreciated." Then if you don't hear within a month, I think you are justified in picking up the phone to make an inquiry. Ask the question. "Are you interested in buying my article?" You can explain that your article subject matter is timely. You'd like to know if the editor has read it—yet.

In making telephone calls to editorial offices, be diplomatic. Avoid jumping down the throat of the unsuspecting soul who answers your call. Say you want to be sure the mail carrier delivered your manuscript. (You can always blame the post office; they're used to it.)

If, in spite of all efforts to nudge the editorial office into awareness of just how important your article is, you're still left waiting, you always have the option of asking that your manuscript be withdrawn from consideration and returned. Be firm, polite, and businesslike. You're a professional, remember?

There it is. In today's competitive world, good market research and procedures are more important than ever. You have a product you want to sell. To sell, you must give your product the best packaging (neatness of manuscript) and make sure it has something other similar products don't have. Something new and different—a fresh twist on an old idea, or an exciting *new* idea other writers haven't found yet.

Research your markets thoroughly. Make sure your article goes to the right one. If you do these things, you'll have a good chance of selling what you write, as so many other writers have done.

When you do make that first sale, or 100th sale, I want to know about it. Write me % Writer's Digest Books. The address: 9933 Alliance Road, Cincinnati, OH 45242.

The Best
of All Worlds—
In Business for
Yourself

I n calling attention to Small Business Week in America, the editor of my local paper began his editorial as follows:

Small businesses provide the steam to propel the American economy into the future.

He then described how Thomas Edison began his career in a home laboratory, and how Orville and Wilbur Wright launched their experiments in flight in their home bicycle shop. Henry Ford's garage was so small a wall had to be knocked out to get his first automobile into the street. And Hewlett and Packard, two engineering students, started their electronic business in a home workshop.

The editorial said that more and more enterprising people are engaged in cottage industries with a wide variety of products and services pouring into the marketplace from the garage workbench, the kitchen table, and the family den. Among this increasing number of home businesses is that of the freelance writer.

If you're one of this hard-working brigade, the stay-at-home-writer, consider the area where you work as hallowed ground, whether it be the cleared-off kitchen table, the broom closet, or, lucky you, a room exclusively set aside for your writing.

When you close the door on your office, in actuality or symbolically, you will be there for a specified time with a job to do—just as though you were a banker, a brain surgeon, a dress shop owner, or a teacher. What you do is important and your time and space deserve to be respected.

Sometimes a writer unknowingly brings derision on himself. He doesn't take himself seriously, and so others treat him and his efforts lightly. In spite of putting out as much physical energy in a day as a hod carrier, to say nothing of the great mental energy required in creative effort, too many writers, like Rodney Dangerfield, "don't get no respect."

It's hard to respect anyone with a poor self-image. The writer who sings the blues perpetually, blaming editors, the market condition, his family, his nine-to-five job for his lack of success can expect only pity from friends and relatives, certainly not respect.

Admittedly, writers are in a vulnerable position with so little to show for their efforts in the first, second, and third draft stages of writing. How can you impress anyone with pages in which words are crossed out, paragraphs slashed through, and margins strewn with notations?

"I can hardly read this myself," the writer laments to the friend looking over his shoulder. The on-looker murmurs some polite remark to the effect that writing must be "interesting."

If you want to avoid the pain of such a scene, don't show your work to anyone except other professional writers, the only ones who can see the nuggets of gold glittering in the muck of mud.

TOOLING UP

1. *Your business.* Think of yourself as a business person at all times.

2. *Your office.* Wherever you work is your office. Treat it as such, furnishing it adequately with a desk or worktable, a comfortable chair, a portable or stationary file, and one or two shelves for your reference books.

You can find reasonably priced office furniture at second-hand outlets. It is just as important for you to make the decision to invest as much money as you can in your writing business as it would be if you were investing in any other kind of business. If you wanted to take tennis lessons, you'd certainly need a good racket. You've decided you want to be a professional writer, and with that commitment should go the realization that there are and will be expenses.

The actual physical location of your "office" isn't as important as is your attitude toward yourself when you're in that special place. Wherever you write, think of yourself as a professional doing an important job.

My desk consists of two closet doors, taken down and

trimmed to fit the specifications I need. One door rests on my two 28½-inch-tall filing cabinets, each containing two file drawers. My printer rests atop one door, and my word processor the other. My typewriter is on what once was a sewing table. My books are shelved on either side of me.

I facetiously refer to my office as having two departments—the typing pool, and the word processing department. I only have to swing my rotating chair around to move from one to the other.

For years, I worked (wrote) on the dining room table, clearing away coloring books and crayons left by my two small sons, and the vestiges of the last meal. Many of my confession stories and my five early romance novels were typed out on that table. As I look back on clearing away the table to make room for my writing, I remember those days as some of the happiest in my life.

Now I have a room in which to write, my office. The *physical* location has changed, but not the attitude. Wherever I write, I'm completely absorbed in what I do. When my husband retires, we'll spend much of our time at our mountain cabin. Back to writing on the dining room table I'll go, and while I'm there that space will be my office—the place where I *work*.

3. *Your typewriter.* This expense, I feel, deserves special consideration. You'll live with your typewriter day after day for years. A typewriter is a hard-working part of your writing team and deserves your loving care. The day when writers cranked out best sellers on broken-down machines is long gone. Editors expect clear, sharp, neat copy. Most editors will accept machine copies, but only if they are good ones. You can't get good copy from hard-to-read typewritten text.

Spend as much as you can afford on your typewriter. Watch the ads in your local newspaper for good buys. Schools and government offices often have auction sales on all kinds of office equipment, including typewriters. Secondhand stores, even flea markets, are outlets for good typewriter buys, but take someone knowledgeable along with you to make sure you won't buy someone else's problems.

Keep your typewriter in good repair and take it to a recognized service center for repair. Good maintenance pays off when the time comes that you're ready to trade in your old friend for a new model.

Buy *at least* two typewriter ribbons at a time. There is nothing more frustrating than to have the ribbon snarl up or become so ragged you can't use it just when you're really rolling. At such a time, who wants to get in the car and tootle down to the store to get a new ribbon? If you have an extra on hand at all times, you stop production for only a minute to make the ribbon change.

4. *Your word processor?* If you haven't done so already, you may be thinking of trading in your typewriter for a word processor. A word of caution: I have a word processor but I didn't get rid of my trusty typewriter. Writer friends warned me that I'd still have occasions when I would prefer the typewriter to the word processor, and they were right. Even though I am fairly comfortable with the word processor after a year's use, I still like to use my typewriter for correspondence. I save my word processor and printer for the important work of creating and printing up manuscripts for publication.

If the day is stormy and there's a chance of our electric current going off, I turn to the typewriter with a sense of security. (If the current went off while I was using the word processor, I could lose a disk's worth of material.) If I'm traveling and have a deadline or want to continue writing on the road, I take my typewriter.

If you haven't bought a word processor but are thinking of investing in one, I'd strongly urge you to shop around with a friend who already has one. Talk to several writers who work on a word processor. Read the monthly columns in *Writer's Digest* on the subject of word processing, written by different contributors. Read magazines that specialize on information relative to computers and word processing, such as *Family Computing.*

More and more writers are opting for the word processor. I am more than happy with mine, and feel it has saved me hours and hours of time in not having to retype, because I can make all kinds of revisions right on the screen before the printer magically goes to work and spills out nearly perfect copy. My typewriter and printer match each other in print and so I can make small corrections on copy from the printer right on my typewriter.

5. *Your telephone.* Whoever heard of a busy office without a telephone? Wherever yours is located in your home, consider it a part of your office. Use it to make contacts with people who can help you in your business: your reference librarian, your Chamber of Commerce public relations person, your historical society, your post office, and so forth.

If you can afford an answering machine, get one. It will save you the frustration of jumping up and down to answer calls, most of which could wait.

6. *Your paper supplies.* All kinds of businesses run on paper. In the business of writing, paper products are an absolute necessity. Buy good quality, sixteen- or twenty-pound bond for your final drafts. Less expensive, colored typing paper is OK for first, second, and third drafts. Typing paper of any color should be in standard size for a writer, 8½ x 11. Buy in quantity if you can. It will save you money. Watch for sales.

You'll need a generous supply of envelopes in all sizes from small letter size to 8½ x 11 and 9 x 12. Whenever you write any kind of correspondence relative to your business, include a self-addressed, stamped envelope for reply. When sending a manuscript, be sure to include a large enough return envelope.

7. *Your reference books.* Start your writer's library today if you haven't done so already. Reference books are a matter of personal interest, but all writers need the basics, such as a good standard dictionary, a book of quotations, an almanac, an atlas, a book of synonyms, etc., a style manual and a thesaurus.

You'll find a bibliography of reference books and titles of books on writing at the end of this book. I've tagged my favorites, books that have helped me do a better job over the years.

To save yourself money, join *Writer's Digest Book Club* and other book clubs to get the discount allowed to members.

8. *Your magazines.* Have a budget and a place in your office area allotted for your supply of monthly magazines. Again, you'll find a list of magazines helpful to writers at the back of this book.

A word of advice concerning magazines. Avoid the pack-rat compulsion—piles and piles of old yellowing magazines gathering dust in a closet or a garage awaiting the day when you think you'll run through them to clip and save various articles. Such clutter is a space-taker and a time-waster. When you see an article that interests you, one you could use in some research project, clip it and then file it as soon as possible. I keep one basket marked TO FILE, into which I toss my clipped articles until I find a convenient time for filing.

9. *Your files.* There are many filing systems. You may have to experiment until you find the one that suits you best. I favor manila folders labeled according to subject matter.

You may have several general classifications under which you file. I have four file drawers under my desk. The first drawer is marked, NONFICTION. During the writing of this book, I kept eight file folders, each related to the article types discussed. In addition, I have folders on many other subjects related to the writing of nonfiction, such as EDITORIAL CORRESPONDENCE, THE BUSINESS OF WRITING, MARKETING, WORD PROCESSING, and so forth. I also have a folder labeled, ARTICLE IDEAS, into which I drop anything and everything that might trigger an article. When I have time, I go through this folder and refile the accumulation under appropriate headings, such as Retirement, Careers, Relationships, Medicine, Houses, Travel, and Historical Events. Frequently, I add headings as my interest expands.

You'll have your own interests, which will fall into different categories as mine do. If you keep your file folders labeled according to your key interests, you can always find the material you need to write an article on the subject.

Another way to file is to label your file folders according to article types, as I filed the material for the chapters in this book. If you haven't set up files as yet, this is a good place to begin. Start your filing system with folders labeled to match the titles of the chapters in this book.

The important element in maintaining a good filing system is not so much the system you use as it is the effectiveness of your files. If you can put your fingers on a file folder containing material you need *now*, your system works. If you have to paw through a clutter and you only find the wanted item after frustrating hours of search, the system is wrong.

Whatever kind of filing system you use, update it from time to time—once a year, at least.

People and places change. Buildings disappear and new ones rise out of the rubble. Highways and roads are rerouted, leaving Main Street far behind. Even scientific theory changes, as do medical beliefs. As a writer, you must keep abreast of today's discoveries; not yesterday's.

With few exceptions, I'd feel safe in saying that most clippings are useless if you haven't referred to them in a two-year time span. To inspire yourself to get rid of moldy deadwood, read *Clutter's Last Stand*, by Don Aslett (Writer's Digest Books). I was so inspired after reading the book, I went through my files like the white tornado.

I said earlier that I have four file drawers under my desk.

The second drawer contains file folders related to my teaching and is so labeled. Instead of letting copies of *Writer's Digest* and *The Writer* push against the ceiling, I clip the articles I think will most interest my students and file them according to the individual technique—for fiction, articles on characterization, dialogue, viewpoint, conflict, plot, etc.; for nonfiction, my folders are labeled according to article types and related subjects.

My third file drawer is labeled MANUSCRIPTS TO BE REVISED, and the fourth drawer is where I keep folders on general research—subjects not related to writing technique.

In addition to my sturdy file drawers, I also like to keep card indexes with file boxes labeled to correspond with my file-drawer label. The card indexes are handy for brief entries.

Good business practices mean good organization—a place for everything and everything in its place. Well, most of the time anyway. A certain amount of office clutter indicates activity and production. A tidied up office is a luxury we writers can afford only when company's coming.

10. *Your taxes.* Keep a good record of the money you spend to maintain your writing, as any other business person does. Postage, paper supplies, paper clips, typewriter ribbons all add up and can all be taken off your income tax once you qualify as a working writer. Keep account of your submissions to various publications and the response you get, even if it's a rejection slip. Such an accounting is proof to the tax man that you are a producing writer. If there's a doubt in your mind as to what you can deduct and how much you can deduct, consult your IRS office and get the latest facts. Rules for deductions are constantly changing from year to year.

ABOUT TIME!

Time is as much a commodity as are the physical properties of your office. The way time is used is as vital to the success of any business venture as the way money is dispersed.

Time and money are very similar. They both require a certain amount of bookkeeping. To stay on top financially, you must know how much money you have at a given time and then you must allot portions of that money to the things you consider important. If you blow your allotted portion of money on one desire, you won't have any left for the other necessities. The way in which you manage your money makes the difference between struggling to survive and enjoying security.

The way in which you, as a writer, manage your *time* spells the difference between reaching your goal of continued publication and the frustration of writing but never selling.

We all have exactly the same number of hours in each day—twenty-four. We all have responsibilities to others that consume a number of those hours. I don't know any writers, successful or unsuccessful, who don't have commitments that use a measure of each day's time for something other than writing. Most successful writers I know have family obligations and jobs they go to, either part-time or full-time. On a national scale, only a small portion of publishing writers devote all their time to writing.

My own life is fragmented by family and by my teaching, and by the time and energy it takes to promote my book, *Writing Romance Fiction.* I also do a number of workshops throughout the year at various writers' conferences. I tell you this not to win your pity, but to convince you that I *do* understand how difficult it is sometimes to find hours in a day in which to write.

Writer's Digest School gives the following timesaver suggestions to writing students enrolling in its many courses. WDS has given me permission to share them with you.

10 TIMESAVERS FOR FREELANCE WRITERS

1. Get up forty-five minutes earlier than you usually would and spend at least thirty minutes of that on your freelance work.
2. If you're the late-starter type, set aside the same forty-five minutes at the end of the day.
3. Set aside at least one lunch hour per week to "brown-bag" it and concentrate on your research or writing.
4. If you're home-bound and have children to feed every day, offer to trade off with another writer or good friend who has children for an hour or two of uninterrupted quiet once a week. Those 50-100 hours can be crucial to your freelance work.
5. If you can reach your job on public transportation, use it, so that your eyes can be on a notepad or research source instead of the highway.
6. If you work at home, let your friends know that you prefer *not* to be called before X P.M. or between certain hours, since that's when you're at work on your writing.
7. Set aside outside "leg work" days for combined interviewing, research, calls, library work, etc., and save actual writing time to be done uninterrupted in your home office.
8. Use a portable tape recorder in your car on the way to work or on errands; talk a few pages while you drive.

9. If you know you're going to spend an hour in a doctor or dentist's waiting room, take some writing-related work with you.
10. *Never* say to yourself: "Well, I only have an hour—it's not worth getting started for that little time." One hundred such hours in 365 days can mean a lot to your freelancing efforts.

With the Timesavers in mind, decide which hours of the day are best for you to write. Only you can make this important decision. Imagine for the moment that you are considering going to work for someone else. Ask yourself a few pertinent questions before you take the job.

1. Do you prefer the day shift, or the night shift?
2. Do you want a full-time job, or are you only interested in part-time employment?
3. Do you have other obligations, such as small children who need your care during certain hours of the day? If so, can you write with them underfoot? If not, can you arrange to have someone else take them off your hands an hour or two a day while you write?
4. Is the rest of your family in agreement that it's OK for you to take this job which will require your total concentration during a specified time each day?
5. Are you excited about this job? Are you willing to give it your all (time) in hopes of advancement and increase in pay?

Only by answering these questions honestly can you hope to succeed as a writer. What time of day is best for you to write? There are early birds who rise with the sun, grab a cup of coffee and a piece of toast and rush to their typewriters to get in an hour or two of writing before they tackle their other day chores—whether it be getting the family off to school and to work, or going off to a job themselves.

One of my students is a clinical psychologist with a daily case load of patients to counsel.

"I love the early morning hours," says Ron. "That's when I'm at my best."

"Not I," chimes in Laura, another student. "It takes me a couple of hours to get going. It's nine o'clock before I sit down to write."

Still another student finds the hours after the family is bedded down the best time to write. "The house is quiet then," explains Jim. "There's no television blasting away. The telephone doesn't ring. Sometimes I write from ten or eleven P.M. until one or two A.M."

These are the part-time writers who must grab whatever they can out of a day filled with an eight-to-five job, a job necessary to put beans on the table while they wait for their writing to pay off.

Full-time writers differ as much as part-timers when it comes to a discussion as to which is the best time to write. Most of the professional full-time writers I know put in the equivalent of an eight-hour day at least five days a week. Many work even longer hours.

When you make the decision of how much time you can give your writing, whether part-time or full-time, set realistic goals. It's better to assign a small portion of each day to your writing and *make it,* than it is to struggle against impossible odds by reaching for time that just isn't there.

ABOUT DETERMINATION

What part-time writers lack in time they make up for in dedication. As a writing teacher, I am constantly amazed at the amount of writing many of my students cram into little dabs of time. The few who lament, "I don't have time to write," often change their tune when they see how much their classmates accomplish, writing part-time.

The complaint, "I don't have time to write," is often just a defense. The writer who sings this sad tune could be afraid of failing, or is not yet ready to make the commitment to spend scarce free time at the typewriter. It's still more fun to go shopping, to play golf or bridge, or to curl up with a book someone else has written.

If you were an employer interviewing someone for a job, would you hire anyone not sure of getting to the plant or office at the required time each day and staying there until the whistle blows at closing time? Hardly. Unless the house catches on fire or some physical calamity occurs, employees are expected to be on the job during working hours and to turn out a certain amount of work each day. If they fail to meet this contract, they find themselves replaced in short order.

When you "hire on" as a writer, whether you work part-time or full-time, sign a contract with yourself as you would sign one for any employer. For whatever time you agree to work, you'll be at your desk writing. If committing yourself to a rigid schedule of so many hours a day is too much for you, physically or psychologically, then be a "piece" worker. Sign an agreement with yourself to write so many pages per day.

One of my students travels sixty-five miles once a week to come to my class, after working a full day in a day-care center for preschool children. When I ask, as I always do, "Well, did you write this week?" Diane answers, "Yes. I did my five pages." Five pages don't seem like many to accomplish in a week, but those five pages are the equivalent of a good dramatic scene in the young adult novel she's writing. Her book is moving forward. It's not standing still.

One page a day equals 365 pages a year—the equivalent of a short novel, a nonfiction book, or several short stories or articles. It makes no difference whether you count your day's effort in hours or pages. The important thing is to realize that you can't be a writer without being on the job—any more than you could be a doctor without going to the hospital or clinic, or an actor without appearing on stage or before the cameras.

In making a commitment to write as much as you can *when you can,* realize you'll have to make a sacrifice. Many of the pleasurable activities—bowling, coffee klatches, shopping sprees, long telephone conversations—will have to be erased from your schedule to allow time for your writing. If becoming involved in any of these enjoyable activities cuts into your writing time, you must be firm with yourself and give them up. If that seems cruel and harsh, remember that you couldn't take time off from any other job to go bowling, golfing, or to visit with friends.

There are certain obligations you can't sidestep. You can't write well if your mind isn't at peace concerning the welfare of your loved ones. Children must be given time and care. Spouses expect more than a vacant stare. You can't put the people you love into a closet and slam the door until you're ready to let them out.

It is possible, however, to make arrangements for your family that leave you with a certain number of hours to write. You can trade off baby-sitting hours with a neighbor or with another writer. If your children are beyond the baby-sitting stage, give them housekeeping responsibilities and make them a part of your team.

While it is true that family and friends should leave you alone during your writing time, it is important to share other parts of your writing life with those you love. There is nothing sadder than a "closet writer," a writer who feels compelled to sneak away and write because someone might laugh, or worse, resent the hours spent writing. A writer needs family support, understanding, and encouragement.

In the early days of a writer's career, when sales are far between and rejection is the order of the day, it may be hard to convince your family that anything will come of your effort.

Remember, all it takes to change the climate from cool interest (or even hostile response) to fevered applause is a few checks in the mail. When you start selling and publishing, the family will come running.

In the meantime, to "get respect," to avoid being a Rodney Dangerfield clone, be businesslike about your writing. Treat it with the respect it deserves. Act like a professional with a proper place and a convenient (for you) time in which you keep "office" hours.

In making the commitment to become a published writer, make sure the job is one you really want. Can you take rejection? Can you tolerate hours of isolation? If you never published anything you wrote, would you still feel compelled to go to your typewriter or word processor whenever you could manage the time?

If you can honestly answer yes to these questions, you're in business. If you have yet to make it, to publish, don't worry. Chances are good you'll eventually find a buyer.

Don't be discouraged by long dry spells when nothing you write seems to get editorial interest. Among my colleagues are many who have waited years to realize their writing goals, suffering many disappointments before the big break came.

Cecilia Bartholomew, a respected writer-friend, is an example of how important it is to keep the faith. Cecilia wrote a short story years ago about incest. The world wasn't ready for that subject then, and the story was rejected many times. Years later when the world had broadened its view of the sensitive areas of life, Cecilia's story made publishing history after she developed the idea from short story to novel form. The novel, titled *Outrun the Dark,* was published by Doubleday with a five-figure advance, became a best seller, was made into a movie, and then became a television drama. Cecilia's idea had found its own time. Again, perseverance paid off.

Publisher's Row is filled with stories of rejected novels, short stories, and articles that finally received the attention they deserved. Irving Stone's *Lust for Life* was turned down twenty times before acceptance. *The Caine Mutiny* also had many turn-downs before finding a publisher. Barnaby Conrad sold a short story to *Esquire* after thirteen rejections. The message is, DON'T GIVE UP! Every business has its ups and downs, *bonanzas* and *borascas,* as the Spanish call them; good days and bad ones.

Every smart businessman tries to make his product salable, changing design, colors, and packaging. Merchandisers experiment with different locations for their products in a department. Perhaps a shift to center aisle might be better. The writer who wants to publish must be as ready to modify, change, add on, and take away, when it comes to the marketing of his product.

BONUS BENEFITS

In addition to the advantages of self-employment that were discussed earlier in this chapter, the rewards for good writing and astute marketing are many. There is always the possibility of riches and fame. Then there are the *intangibles*, the returns that have little to do with money or recognition.

One of the greatest rewards that comes with being a writer is the number of stimulating people you meet when you attend writers' conferences, classes, and workshops. New writers attending their first writers' event are often amazed at the warm rapport and the generosity of writers who freely share market news, editorial letters, and their own expertise. Very few writers are stingy with their hard-won knowledge; most want to help one another.

A support system is important to a writer. When the going gets tough, only another writer can fully understand. Lasting friendships are certainly to be counted among the rewards. Another fringe benefit that compensates for long hours of solitary toil is the total absence of discrimination as to age, race, and economic status. Writers have such a strong common bond that barriers in other worlds cease to exist in the writing world. The important question is always, "What are you writing now?" Your age and the color of your hair or skin do not matter. All that matters is what you're writing.

A final reward is the exciting challenge of each day when you go to your typewriter, roll in a sheet of paper, and create whole new worlds of thought, ideas other people never dream of until you breathe life into them in your writing.

Is it any wonder that all kinds of people want to be writers—movie stars, doctors, politicians, athletes, the mother who stays at home caring for her youngsters?

The truth is, there *are* more people getting into the writing profession every day. You only have to turn on your television to see someone, unknown yesterday, now promoting his or her book. The competition has never been quite so fierce. Competition makes you work harder. When you work harder, you become a better writer. In spite of competition, new writers do break into publishing. Competition *is* good for business.

Once More with Feeling— Final Thoughts

B efore leaving you, there are some personal thoughts I'd like to share with you, thoughts that go beyond the techniques I've given you for learning to write and sell the easiest article types.

Understanding the various techniques used by successful writers to write and sell in the nonfiction field is vitally important to your success. It would be virtually impossible to arrive at Publisher's Row without knowing the elements that provide the foundation for article writing. Once you understand the purpose of each technique or "building block," you can begin to channel your ideas into salable articles for a wide variety of markets.

As with any other endeavor, practice makes for smooth professional performance. The more you write, the better you write; that is, if you learn the rules and follow them.

Can you ever break the rules?

You certainly can, but only after you *know* the rules and the purpose for which they were created. Those who never take the time to learn the rules break them unknowingly, and the result is failure. Those who learn the rules and use them to insure professionalism in their writing sometimes break the rules, but always with a purpose and not out of ignorance.

Truman Capote broke the rules when he wrote, *In Cold Blood,* creating a new format combined of the best elements of nonfiction mixed with the dramatic elements of fiction. Capote's new creation became known as *faction*—fact plus fiction. Since *In Cold Blood,* other writers have followed suit, and in books and articles we see more and more of the marriage of nonfiction and fiction.

To go beyond the rules, to reach out for new horizons in creativity, is the hallmark of a master craftsman in any of the arts. It takes courage to break tried and tested ways of doing things. And it takes something more—experience.

Until you know beyond a certainty that you can write and sell the kinds of articles you like to write while obeying the rules, I suggest you delay far-out innovations. Truman Capote was a well-established writer with many publishing credits in fiction and nonfiction before he decided to put *In Cold Blood* into *faction.* He had proved himself as a writer to the publishing and reading world.

So should you.

If you haven't published as yet, go back to one of the article types that appealed to you. Read the chapter on that particular kind of article several times. Do the suggested exercise, using your notebook to jot down ideas. Answer the questions pertaining to the testing of your idea to make sure it fits the article type you've chosen.

Concentrate on this one article type that interests you, using the models you've clipped from various magazines to guide you. Outline your idea, using the suggestions I've given you. Rewrite. Use the check list at the end of the chapter to make sure you've included all the necessary elements needed for that particular kind of article.

If you write and submit a dozen articles in a particular category and you get only rejection slips in return, read the chapter again. Look at the articles you've written with a cold, objective eye. Compare them again to published articles on ideas similar to yours. Another rewrite may be necessary.

Sometimes changing the lead is all that is necessary to turn a reject into a sale. Or perhaps you need more backup material, more examples, more quotations and statistics to support your premise. It could be your ending lacks a strong take-away for the reader. Consider how you could give it more punch, more emotional impact.

When you've looked over your rejected articles with the objectivity that only distance can give, make the necessary revisions and send them out again.

Keep in mind the Carol Amen story and other examples I gave you of how hanging in there paid off for other writers who, like yourself, were rejected—not once but many times.

THE PHILOSOPHY OF THE SUCCESSFUL WRITER

In addition to knowing how to write professionally, using all the elements of technique to best advantage, there's another ingredient you'll need in order to survive the stiff competition on Publisher's Row: You must have an enduring faith in yourself and your ability to write, a faith strong enough to support you through all the ups and downs that are a part of a writer's life. Such a faith is almost a credo, a belief so strong that nothing short of death can wipe it out.

In teaching and in working with hundreds of writers over a period of many years, I've come to recognize this invincible quality, and when I sense its presence in a writer I know that person can't help but succeed. I may lose track of that student for a long time, but eventually I get a letter saying, "Remember that article I wrote in your class? Well, I finally sold it!"

The magic word is "finally." The writer didn't give up. He or she kept on trying and trying, revising, changing, adding, deleting, watching the market news, until one day just the right market came along, with an editor who saw the potential in the piece.

Most writers have long dry spells, times when everything they write seems to draw only the rejection slip instead of that long, slim envelope containing an acceptance and a check, or the promise of one. Most professional writers admit that after so many rejections they do have their moments of depression. They don't allow the depression to linger on too long, however. Faith in their talent drives them back to the typewriter.

Listen to Your Inner Voice

"I know I can do it," the small voice within the writer whispers, refusing to be silenced by rejection. "I know I can do it. What I've written is good. It's every bit as good as the published articles I've been studying. I'll send it out—one more time."

That's what makes the difference. Four little words. I CAN DO IT! And three little words. ONE MORE TIME!

What else do you need to survive as a writer when the going gets tough? Aren't talent, perseverance, and faith enough? Not quite.

YOU NEED A SUPPORT SYSTEM

Writing talent, the ability to breathe life into an idea through the written word, will get you started. Perseverance and faith will keep you going when the returns for your labor are sparse or nil. These ingredients, talent, perseverance, and faith, are an innate part of your writer self. Think of them as members of your team, loyal all the way, eager to serve you with devotion, and always ready to comfort you.

To keep your team together and working for you, you must nurture it so that each member grows stronger and not weaker when the going gets rough. You do this through an outer support system, a network of writer friends who also believe in you.

Who Are Your Writer-Friends?

Supportive writer friends can be members of your family, your writing teacher, and colleagues who belong to your writing class or club. A supportive writer friend might be someone you've never met face to face, for example, an instructor in a writing course taught through correspondence, such as through the Writer's Digest School, or any other good correspondence school for writing instruction.

Among my Writer's Digest students are many who live in outlying districts where there are no available writing classes, and often no contact with other writers. A correspondence course in such a circumstance becomes a lifeline—the instructor one person out there who understands the need for support during those difficult days of learning and rejection.

If you fall into this category, marooned from contact with writer friends, with no classes or writers' groups near you, think of taking a correspondence course. Make sure that the course is taught by a publishing writer-teacher, someone with interests similar to your own, and someone who is selling to today's markets.

There are many teachers who do a great job of teaching English literature and composition to college students, but such teachers are not always interested in what they think of as "commercial writing," that is, writing to publish for a mass readership of popular magazines. That's why it's important for you who want to sell what you write to find a teacher who has the experience to help you do just that.

Sharing the Wealth—of Experience

Most towns of any size have adult education classes held in various high schools, or community services classes (including writing) often held on college campuses. I've attended and taught in both. Several students who were in my writing classes a few years ago are now teaching those same classes.

Those of you who are publishing regularly might want to think about sharing what you've learned through teaching other struggling writers. If so, you'll be warmly welcomed by adult education school principals and college administrators who are looking for qualified teachers.

Teaching writing brings a very special reward, namely an opportunity to share in the development of creative talent, and perhaps to give that all-important encouragement to someone who needs it desperately.

Teaching writing is a wonderful support for your own creative endeavors, and it can give you a nice little extra income. Glance through the pages of trade publications for writers and you'll be surprised at the number of successful writers who are drawn to the classroom and the smell of chalk dust.

What you give of yourself and your talent in teaching others returns multiplied many times. Seeing others work so hard to make the jump from amateur to professional in the writing field keeps you on your toes. As a teacher, you share in the intimate details of a student's home life, and are aware of the obstacles in his or her path. Such confidences are humbling and make you doubly appreciative of your own good fortune in arriving safely at Publisher's Row.

ENTER THE VILLAIN

No matter how invincible your faith and perseverance, and in spite of a strong outer support system, you can fall victim to a paralyzing condition known as writer's block.

When this psychological ailment strikes you down you're terrified, believing it's a terminal disease. The malady can overtake you with the suddenness of a lightning bolt. The symptoms are unmistakable.

All of a sudden you can't write.

You want to write. There's the typewriter waiting with a fresh ribbon newly installed. There's that nice stack of white manuscript paper. And there's that article awaiting the magic touch of your fertile brain and flying fingers.

Why aren't you in there at the typewriter writing?

Because you've got writer's block. Something has frozen the creative juices. You're overwhelmed with self-doubt. Whom are you trying to kid, thinking you're a great writer? All those pages and pages you wrote yesterday and the day before, and the day before that—they suddenly seem to add up to a big fat zero. May as well throw it in the garbage where it belongs and get out and live life the way other people live it—time for golf, tennis, bridge, shopping.

You think of a thousand other long-neglected activities. Such as cleaning house. You've never been the *Better Homes and Gardens* variety of housekeeper, but suddenly you can't wait to scrub the walls, wash the windows, and attack the cobwebs. Then there's the garden, and the yard.

The things you feel obligated to do now comprise an endless list. If you're smart, you'll heed the call to domestic duty and dig out the broom and cleaning rags, or you'll take off for the golf links, the tennis court, the beach—anywhere away from your typewriter.

The compulsion to do anything except write is Nature's way of telling you that you need to back off from this day-after-day grind of creating and the ordeal of trying to turn out publishable material. Your brain cells need a rest.

The best way to rest the brain is to use the muscles that work the arms and legs. Physical activity in any form is the best medicine for writer's block. A few days chasing cobwebs, washing walls and windows, or digging up the south forty is all the motivation you need to get back to the typewriter.

Ideas that you thought would never come again suddenly surge into your mind as you're using whatever brawn you possess in physical activity. That difficult place in your article suddenly smooths out. You know just what to do. You can't wait to get started again.

If you're not the domestic sort and detest housework, and if plowing and planting leave you cold, there are other cures for writer's block. Here are a few suggestions:

1. Read Don Aslett's *Clutter's Last Stand,* published by Writer's Digest Books. It will inspire you to an all-out attack on those files filled with material past the yellowing stage and turning brown.

2. Write to writer friends, pouring out your woe about writer's block. Corresponding with kindred souls is one of the best medicines I know for writer's blues and writer's block.

3. Catch up on your reading. It won't be long before something another writer has written will inspire you to an idea of your own.

4. Visit a public place where the crowd surges back and forth. Study people's faces. Listen in to bits of conversation. Play the guessing game of wondering where this person and that one are going. Make up stories about different people as they pass you by.

5. Start up a conversation with a stranger. Don't reveal that you're a writer. Ask why this person you've never met and will never see again happens to be living in your area. Where did this stranger live before? What is it this person likes about your town? Dislikes?

The answers to your questions will start the creative juices flowing again. The stranger might come up with an idea about your town that you never thought of before. There might be a dramatic personal experience article in what the stranger tells you, or a bit of nostalgia.

6. Attend a writers' conference. It's impossible not to get inspiration from such an exciting event. Talking with other writers, listening to successful professionals tell how they got their start and how they work is like a transfusion. It rejuvenates your tired brain cells as nothing else could.

At a writers' conference you'll hear other writers tell about the times they were laid low with writer's block, and you'll know you're not alone. Most important, you'll realize it isn't terminal as you thought, but a transient condition that will leave as suddenly as it appeared.

Stay in the Pink

As a writer you subject yourself to stress factors unknown to people in most other occupations. Because you are creative, your antenna is constantly up to receive impulses from the world around you, which in turn stimulates original ideas and concepts. Being constantly bombarded by invisible idea waves can be exhausting.

You've trained yourself to be sensitive to the thoughts and feelings of others so that you'll be able to translate them into your writing. Sometimes this highly developed sensitivity can be emotionally draining. Have you ever had the experience of coming into a room where two people have been quarreling, and although the couple may be all smiles at your appearance, you feel the tension in the air as though it were a living entity? This ability to sense an emotional climate is one small part of the sensitivity so important to writing.

As a writer, you're constantly projecting yourself into the minds and hearts of everyone around you. You feel the joy others experience as though it were your own, and you feel the pain just as intensely. Being creative and stimulated by the vibrations around you can be wearing.

Then there's the wearing effect of sitting at a typewriter or word processor hour after hour. The muscles cramp. Physical fatigue sets in. Sometimes the writer ignores the warning signals and works beyond the healthful limit.

Mental, emotional, and physical stress all take their toll if the warning signals are not heeded. In spite of tales of geniuses working against unbelievable physical handicaps, most of us do our best writing when we feel our best.

Your most treasured asset is your health. Guard it well; take short breaks away from the typewriter or word processor. Go outside and smell the roses. Check the mail box. Do one household or yard chore. Stretch your muscles and your mind. Then return to work refreshed by the little breather you've given yourself. This short break is not the same as the enforced break thrust upon you by writer's block. Decide for yourself when to break and when to return. Discipline yourself to take these breathers from your work and you'll write better for a longer period of time. You can't enjoy what you're doing on any job unless you feel your best.

CONCENTRATION = INSULATION

There is no more demanding work than writing. To be a writer means total concentration in addition to long hours of sitting and typing. To concentrate on an idea and give that idea an identity recognizable to thousands of readers means that you must learn to insulate yourself from outside distractions. These might be trivial, such as a child bouncing a ball near the window, or more serious, such as a domestic crisis.

If you can't change the world around you, you must learn to accept the conditions as they are and create in spite of distractions or obstacles.

In all my years of writing and teaching, I've never met a writer whose world was perfect. Most of the writers I know work, produce, and create in spite of all imaginable obstacles, physical and mental.

If you truly want to be a writer you'll write no matter what the condition in which you find yourself. No circumstance of this world can stop you.

In overcoming obstacles, you'll grow not only as a writer, but as a person, and this growth will enable you to write with better purpose and with greater meaning.

IN CLOSING—HAPPY TALK!

Being a writer isn't all struggle, frustration, and rejection. Few other occupations give the very special sense of triumph and joy that comes to writers when they realize that the idea once spinning around in their brain is now a living thing with an identity, a voice, and a message, with the potential of touching thousands of lives and of changing them in some way.

This moment of incomparable happiness is not measured out to the selling writer only. It comes to the unpublished writer as well. We live in a money world, and pay for labor is necessary and right. Publication, seeing one's name below a title, brings a sense of pride. Most writers want recognition of their talent through publication, and they deserve to be paid for their contributions that fill pages of newspapers, magazines, and books.

Beyond these material considerations—pay and recognition of our talent—is something even greater. It is that private moment when you know you've written something meaningful and good. It may take awhile for others to agree, but you don't care. *You know you can write.* You feel it deep inside you. It's a kind of glow that lights up the darkest places in your writer's world. This is the moment of self-fulfillment. There is no joy quite like it.

My wish for you is that you know many such moments. And you will if you keep in mind these final suggestions:

1. Keep trying to improve your writing.
2. Reach out to people who will provide you with a support system to sustain you during the days of waiting for your dreams to come true.
3. Keep the faith in your God-given talent.

Bibliography

BOOKS RELATED TO THE CRAFT OF WRITING

American Society of Journalists and Authors, The, *Complete Guide to Writing Nonfiction.* Edited by Glen Evans. Cincinnati: Writer's Digest Books, 1983.
> An excellent source of valuable information for writers in all categories, contributed by over 100 professional authors. Part I delves into the provocative subject of what it takes to be a writer, and gives a crash course in the essential elements of good writing. Part II discusses the many facets of the nonfiction market and whether you should specialize or not specialize. Over 800 pages of solid information that no writer can afford to be without. A good companion to *The Beginning Writer's Answer Book.*

Biagi, Shirley, *Write & Sell Magazine Articles.* Englewood Cliffs NJ: Prentice-Hall, 1981.
> A solid little paperback packed with practical suggestions for beginning writers. A good chapter on the writer-photographer, including sources, problems, model releases, etc.

Boggess, Louise, *Writing Fillers That Sell.* Funk & Wagnalls, 1968 first printing.
> Ms. Boggess was one of the pioneers in teaching writing classes when the subject was not as popular in the adult education and college curriculum as it is today. I was privileged to be in one of her classes, and her down-to-earth, no-nonsense approach gave me the direction I needed at the time. *Writing Fillers That Sell* reflects this same approach, and the book will help you get started writing and selling a good door-opener kind of piece— the filler.

Brady John, *The Craft of Interviewing.* Cincinnati: Writer's Digest Books, 1976 first printing.

> A well-thumbed book in my writer's library. Brady not only brings you his expertise on the subject of interviewing from a writer's viewpoint, but also from that of an editor on the staff of *Writer's Digest* and other magazines. From his countless interviews, he shares his own ideas of what to do when you get an assignment to interview and how to avoid some of the pitfalls.

Cassill, Kay, *The Complete Handbook for Freelance Writers.* Cincinnati: Writer's Digest Books, 1981.

> A business book for writers, complete with examples, charts, and sample forms.

Clark, Bernadine, ed., *Writer's Resource Guide.* 2nd edition. Cincinnati: Writer's Digest Books, 1983.

> This book is exactly what the title implies, a guide to hundreds of sources of information on a vast assortment of subjects. Whatever your interest, whatever your research need, this book will tell you where to go and where to write to obtain the information.

Deimling, Paula, ed., *Writer's Market.* Cincinnati: Writer's Digest Books, annually.

> A book that tells you where to sell what you write. Try to update your copy as often as possible, as market addresses change and editors come and go in a musical chair fashion on Publisher's Row. *Writer's Market* is the bible for beginning and established writers in all fields of writing. If you want to know where to send your poem, your column, your short story, your article, your novel, and your nonfiction book, let your fingers walk through the pages of this book.

Duncan, Lois, *How to Write and Sell Your Personal Experiences.* Cincinnati: Writer's Digest Books, 1979.

> I treasure an autographed copy of this book, "For Helene, who

doesn't really need to be told how to do anything! Lois Duncan." Thanks, Lois, but I feel the need to keep learning everything I can about our profession.

Ms. Duncan's opening line hooked me. "Have you ever answered the telephone to hear a strange voice announce that you just won $1,500?" Ms. Duncan then describes how she was awarded the Grand Prize in the *Writer's Digest* Creative Writing Contest. She shows us how she followed that success with many more sales by using her *personal* experiences as the basis of her salable articles.

Emerson, Connie, *Write On Target.* Cincinnati: Writer's Digest Books, 1981.

Ms. Emerson and I share a common theme—the importance of finding out what editors want and need, and then tailoring your ideas to fill the demand.

Freeman, William, compiler, *Dictionary of Fictional Characters.* Revised by Fred Urquhart.

Even if you're not a fiction writer, you should have a first-hand knowledge of the great fictional characters of literature. If you're going to write, "He was a veritable Scrooge," you should know exactly who Scrooge was, where he first appeared. Page 404 tells us that Ebenezer Scrooge was the central character in Dickens's *A Christmas Carol,* which was published in 1843. Scrooge is familiar to most of us, but there are many important less-known fictional characters you may have occasion to track down in the course of your writing. This book will save you hours of detective work.

Hellyer, Clement David, *Making Money With Words.* Englewood Cliffs NJ: Prentice-Hall, 1981.

Mr. Hellyer is another seasoned teacher of writing classes. His style is breezy and entertaining as he takes you on a guided tour through the world of publishing. I found his chapter on writing the how-to book particularly helpful.

Jones, Helen Hinckley, *How to Write and Publish a Step at a Time*. Winell Publishers, 1980.
> Another solid paperback I reread often for inspiration. Ms. Jones is a well-known and much-loved writing teacher on the West Coast. She speaks in her book of the need for a writer to have compassion in order to communicate well. "A writer who has compassion, who really loves people and is concerned with their problems writes warmly even when he writes ineptly," says Jones. I believe that wholeheartedly.

Kredenser, Gail, *Write It Right*. New York: Barnes & Noble, 1972 first printing.
> An inexpensive paperback—to keep at your elbow as you type—on the "art of word watching." This handy guide will tell you how to avoid "juggling words like hot potatoes on paper and allowing your sentences to run out of control." Whether you're writing a letter to the boss requesting a raise in pay or a profound article on curing the ills of the world, this book will help you improve your style and say what you mean. Bothered with split infinitives and a hundred other booby traps of grammar and construction? Read and study *Write It Right*.

Miller, Don. *The Book of Jargon*. New York: Macmillan & Co., 1982.
> If you've ever struggled to interpret the jargon spoken by those who specialize in highly technical fields such as science and medicine, to say nothing of the computer world, you'll find this book a life-saver. It is especially helpful to writers of nonfiction who cover a wide variety of subjects in their articles and must get their background information as quickly as possible. Most helpful in preparing to interview specialists in areas such as medicine, law, real estate, the world of music, and television.

Newcomb, Duane, *How to Make Big Money Free-Lancing*. West Nyack, NJ: Parker Publishing Co., 1970.
> Whenever you feel confused as to just where to send a particular article, this is the book that will clear your head in a hurry.

Newcomb comes right out with the strong statement, "Anyone who can write a clear sentence can make up to $50,000 a year." The success of his many writing students proves his premise. It takes only a glance at a few pages of this dynamic book to get you excited again about a project that may have cooled.

Polking, Kirk, ed., *The Beginning Writer's Answer Book.* Revised and expanded edition. Cincinnati: Writer's Digest Books, 1984.
A quick, ready-reference source of information on a wide variety of subjects related to writing and publishing. The questions are those that constantly plague the beginning writer and often challenge the well-established professional. Questions are answered in a direct and concise way, giving specific information.
I wore out the 1968 edition, bought the 1984 edition, and keep it above my typewriter for fingertip reference when I don't know or when I've forgotten.

Polking, Kirk, ed., *Writer's Encyclopedia.* Cincinnati: Writer's Digest Books, 1983.
A comprehensive reference for students, teachers, writers, and editors. Over 1,000 alphabetical entries, cross-referenced, defining terms in an easy-to-understand way. A good place to start your study of the world of writing.

There are many more books on the craft of good writing that I could list, but space is limited. I hope this sampling will inspire you to start a library of your own favorites, books you'll cart along with you wherever you go, returning to them time and again.

DICTIONARIES AND WORD-FINDERS

Good dictionaries and word-finders are as important to a writer as are the pick and shovel and pan to the gold prospector. Workers in any occupation need tools to get the job done. Words are the writer's tools. To keep them honed and sharp, and to make sure there's the right tool for the right job, frequent referral to dictionaries and word-finders is a *must.*

The following is a suggested list I've found extremely helpful during my writing career.

The American Heritage Dictionary of Misused Words. New York: Dell Publishing Co., 1979.
> A purse-size Dell book. Clear, precise definitions of commonly misused and misspelled words. A life-saver.

Bartlett's Familiar Quotations. Boston: Little, Brown and Co.
> Has given thought wings many times. Whenever I want to know who said what, I turn to Bartlett.

Bernstein, Theodore M., *Reverse Dictionary.* New York: Times Books, 1979.
> Whereas conventional dictionaries list words alphabetically, Bernstein lists *meanings* and then gives you a choice of words. Ideal for when you're groping for a word, can't think of it, but you have a general idea of meaning.
>
> Example: Polo time period: *Chukker*

Foreign Language Phrase Book. New York: Dell Publishing Co., 1982.
> Another Dell mini booklet. Gives the most frequently used phrases found in Spanish, French, German, and Italian.

Grammar for Grown-Ups. New York: Dell Publishing Co., 1981.
> Still another purse-size Dell booklet available in supermarkets, drugstores, and bookstores. Costs less than a dollar. A refresher course in sentence structure, word usage, parts of speech, and punctuation.

Shipley, Joseph T., ed., *Dictionary of World Literary Terms.* Boston: *The Writer,* 1979.
> Want to know what *affectation* means as applied to writing? No? How about *closet drama?* Or *historical present? Literary Terms* tells you exactly what these and hundreds of other words and phrases mean as related to the art of writing. Good background information for all kinds of writing.

Sisson, A.F., *Sisson's Word and Expression Locater.* West Nyack, NJ: Parker Publishing Co., 1966.
> Another book to help you when you know the meaning, but can't think of the word. *Locater* helps you find the word quickly. You supply the meaning and *Locater* finds the word. You can start with a general idea and find many words in this book that will add dimension to your concept.

Strunk, William Jr., and E. B. White, *The Elements of Style.* New York: Macmillan Publishing Co., 1972.
> A bible when it comes to questions of grammar, proper usage.

Webster's Instant Word Guide. Springfield, MA: G.&C. Merriam Co., 1980.
> Hardcover but in smaller than pocketbook size. No meanings or definitions, just correct spelling. Handy for times when you can't remember if *i* comes before *e.*

Webster's New World Dictionary of the American Language,
College Edition. Cleveland and New York: World Publishing
Co., 1960.
>   Well-thumbed and showing hard usage. Has come to the rescue
>   many times.

The Writer's Book of Synonyms and Antonyms. Boston: *The
Writer,* 1971.
>   More than 5,000 key words with selection of synonyms and an-
>   tonyms. A good vocabulary builder. Saves you when it comes
>   to difficult choice of just the *right* word.

Other helpful little Dell purse booklets for writers are: *How to
Read Faces Instantly* (1978), *3000 Uncommon Names for
Baby* (1976), and *The Book of Pet Names* (1978). Look for
these tiny booklets near your check-out stand at your favorite
supermarket.

OTHER HELPFUL REFERENCE BOOKS

Travel

Doubleday, Nelson, and C. Early Cooley, eds., *Encyclopedia of
World Travel.* 2 vols. New York: Doubleday & Co., 1961.

Triple A (AAA) Travel Books. Published by the American Automobile Association, Falls Church, VA.
>   Cover any state or country you're interested in. Marvelous
>   guides to planning your travel writing—as well as your vaca-
>   tions. These books are updated yearly.

Zobel, Louise Purwin, *The Travel Writer's Handbook.* Cincinnati: Writer's Digest Books, 1980.
>   Everything you need to know about writing your travel experi-
>   ences.

In this category, the *Fodor's* and *Sunset* travel guides, as well as travel books published by Time-Life Books, are also helpful.

History

Great Events of the 20th Century—How They Changed Our Lives. Pleasantville, NY: Reader's Digest, 1982.
> Reader's Digest Almanac and Yearbook—Updated yearly. Older editions still useful.

The *Old West* Series. Alexandria, VA: Time-Life Books. Includes *The Soldiers, The Miners, The Cowboys, The Trailblazers, The Indians,* and *The Railroads.*
> Published in a series during the early 1970s.

Reader's Digest Almanac and Yearbook. Pleasantville, NY. Updated yearly.
> Older editions still useful.

This Fabulous Century. Alexandria, VA: Time-Life Books.
> Covers 1870-1890 up to the present decade. Everything you need to know to write about people and events in the past. Fascinating reading. Good for nostalgia research.

Self-Improvement

Aslett, Don, *Clutter's Last Stand.* Cincinnati: Writer's Digest Books, 1984.
> I was so inspired by this book on how to rid your life, your relationships, and your files of useless accumulation that I immediately cleared out three file drawers of aging material turning brown. The humor and common sense in this book will turn any writer on. Should be required reading of all pack rats.

Bowling, Evelyn Burge, *Voice Power.* Harrisburg, PA: Stackpole Books, 1980.
> A must for any writer who takes to the podium or lecture platform. How to improve your voice and your delivery. Power speeches and sales presentations.

Rosenbaum, Jean, M.D., and Veryl Rosenbaum, Psa, *The Writer's Survival Guide—How to Cope with Rejection, Success, and 99 Other Hang-Ups of the Writing Life.* Cincinnati: Writer's Digest Books,1982.
> Fine source of motivation for writers, explaining many of the hang-ups that can hold a writer back and giving encouraging suggestions for handling rejection.

BOOKS TO INSPIRE AND MOTIVATE

Gentz, William, Lee Roddy, and others, *Writing to Inspire.* Cincinnati: Writer's Digest Books, 1982.
> Backup from 30 leading inspiration writers. Shows you the ins and outs of writing for the growing religious market.

Knott, Leonard L., *Writing for the Joy of It.* Cincinnati: Writer's Digest Books, 1983.
> The title says it all—whether you're interested in the professional approach or in writing as a hobby. The author shows you the many ways in which you can use your talent for your own self-satisfaction. "Anything else is a bonus," Knott says.

Murphy, Dr. Joseph, *The Power of Your Subconcious Mind.* Englewood Cliffs, NJ: Prentice-Hall, 1963 first printing. Many reprints.
> This book is a good answer to "writer's block," when for reasons you don't understand, you seem to run dry. Your subcon-

scious mind is a powerful treasure chest, the source of creativity. This book shows you how to draw upon it so that you use your full potential of talent and creativity.

Perret, Gene, *How to Hold Your Audience with Humor.* Cincinnati: Writer's Digest Books, 1984.
>Gene Perret is a comedy writer for many of the top funny men of radio and television. A must for published writers facing the lecture platform.

TRADE PUBLICATIONS

Writer's Digest
9933 Alliance Road
Cincinnati, Ohio 45242

The Writer
120 Boyston Street
Boston, MA 02116

Publishers Weekly
R. R. Bowker Co.
1911 Rolland Street
Riverton, NJ 08077

Writers Connection
10601 S De Anza Blvd., Suite 301
Cupertino, Ca 95014

Index

Other Books of Interest

General Writing Books
Beginning Writer's Answer Book, edited by Kirk Polking $14.95
Getting the Words Right: How to Revise, Edit, and Rewrite, by Theodore A. Rees Cheney $13.95
How to Become a Bestselling Author, by Stan Corwin, $14.95
How to Get Started in Writing, by Peggy Teeters $10.95
How to Write a Book Proposal, by Michael Larsen $9.95
If I Can Write, You Can Write, by Charlie Shedd $12.95
Knowing Where to Look: The Ultimate Guide to Research, by Lois Horowitz $16.95
Law & the Writer, edited by Polking & Meranus (paper) $9.95
The 29 Most Common Writing Mistakes & How to Avoid Them, by Judy Delton $9.95
Writer's Block & How to Use It, by Victoria Nelson $12.95
Writer's Encyclopedia, edited by Kirk Polking $19.95
Writer's Market, $19.95
Writer's Resource Guide, edited by Bernadine Clark $16.95
Writing From the Inside Out, by Charlotte Edwards (paper) $9.95

Magazine/News Writing
Complete Guide to Writing Nonfiction, edited by The American Society of Journalists & Authors $24.95
How to Write & Sell the 8 Easiest Article Types, by Helene Schellenberg Barnhart $14.95
Magazine Writing: The Inside Angle, by Art Spikol $12.95

Fiction Writing
Fiction Is Folks: How to Create Unforgettable Characters, by Robert Newton Peck $11.95
Fiction Writer's Market, edited by Jean Fredette $17.95
Handbook of Short Story Writing, edited by Dickson and Smythe (paper) $6.95
Storycrafting, by Paul Darcy Boles $14.95
Writing Romance Fiction—For Love and Money, by Helene Schellenberg Barnhart $14.95
Writing the Novel: From Plot to Print, by Lawrence Block $10.95

Special Interest Writing Books
Complete Book of Scriptwriting, by J. Michael Straczynski $14.95
The Craft of Lyric Writing, by Sheila Davis $16.95
How to Write a Cookbook and Get It Published, by Sara Pitzer, $15.95
How to Write a Play, by Raymond Hull $13.95
How to Write & Sell (Your Sense of) Humor, by Gene Perret $12.95
How to Write "How-To" Books and Articles, by Raymond Hull (paper) $8.95
How to Write the Story of Your Life, by Frank P. Thomas $12.95
On Being a Poet, by Judson Jerome $14.95
Poet's Handbook, by Judson Jerome $11.95
TV Scriptwriter's Handbook, by Alfred Brenner (paper) $9.95
Travel Writer's Handbook, by Louise Zobel (paper) $8.95
Writing for Children & Teenagers, by Lee Wyndham (paper) $9.95
Writing for the Soaps, by Jean Rouverol $14.95

The Writing Business
Complete Guide to Self-Publishing, by Tom & Marilyn Ross $19.95
Complete Handbook for Freelance Writers, by Kay Cassill $14.95
Freelance Jobs for Writers, edited by Kirk Polking (paper) $7.95
How You Can Make $20,000 a Year Writing, by Nancy Edmonds Hanson (paper) $6.95

To order directly from the publisher, include $1.50 postage and handling for 1 book and 50¢ for each additional book. Allow 30 days for delivery.
Writer's Digest Books, Dept. B, 9933 Alliance Rd., Cincinnati OH 45242
Prices subject to change without notice.